MARK H NEWHOUSE

The Devil's Bookkeepers Book 2: The Noose Tightens

Newhouse Creative Group

First published by NCG Key 2019

First edition

This book was professionally typeset on Reedsy. Find out more at reedsy.com

Dear Reader

T his is the sequel to *The Devil's Bookkeepers 1: The Noose*. While Book 2 stands alone, I recommend you read Book 1 to learn the origins of this suspenseful story about love, friendship, and courage, in a time of terror. This dramatic series closely follows the timeline of the tightening of the Nazi noose that took place in the Lodz Ghetto in Poland, beginning in 1941, as described in the *Chronicle of the Lodz Ghetto*, edited by Lucjan Dobroszycki, (Yale University Press, 1984). Some character names are real, while most attributes, conversations, and actions are fictitious since little is known about the authors who wrote this record of the suffering, they and those they loved, experienced. The dialogue incorporates some of their anonymous entries and represents my attempt to imagine their responses to the extraordinary circumstances they struggled to overcome. While the characters' behaviors and relationships are figments of my imagination, unfortunately, the historical facts are real. If only we had recordings of what was said as the nightmare unfolded around them.

Some chapters open with *Chronicle* excerpts. Thank you Yale University Press for allowing me to use these. I've chosen to retain their wording, tone, and even errors, to preserve the 'chill factor' as people vanished without explanation, and hope flared only to be extinguished by terrible uncertainty. Of approximately two hundred thousand human beings who suffered in the Lodz ghetto, less than five thousand survived despite the controversial efforts of the ghetto Chairman. Two of these survivors were my parents. I dedicate this

1

work to them, the grandparents and relatives I never knew, and all victims of hate and genocide past, present, and future. The Holocaust is not only about Jews during World War 2, but a warning and call for tolerance that must echo for all time to all people. I hope this story will inspire you to read the original *Chronicle*, written under the noses of the Nazis.

The Holocaust is the shadow that haunted my life. I hope this story has that effect on you, so we may all say,

"Never again to anyone."

Mark, 2019

CHAPTER 1

Poland, the Lodz Ghetto

AFTER MIDNIGHT, JANUARY 1, 1942

A man was shot by a sentry near the barbed wire on Zgierska Street. The sentry had been drinking, but claimed the Jew was trying to escape. It was determined the deceased man was mentally disturbed. No charges were filed against the sentry.

Where would my wife's lover go? The barbed wire sealed off the ghetto, a slum fenced in by the Nazis to house nearly one hundred and fifty thousand Jews. Why? Nobody knew. The bitter cold night woke my senses. I was grateful to be out of our rat-hole and away from Miriam, my young wife. The thought of her betrayal with Singer aroused my fury again.

"Focus. Be logical. Engineer, be logical." Logic would have warned me to go back inside our squalid one-room flat, swallow my hurt and pretend I knew nothing of what Singer had planned. Let him try to escape. He deserves his fate. Why should I, the cuckold, risk my life for him? His note to Miriam, his confession of love, for her, and our child, was burning my heart, poisoning my thoughts. How could they betray me? He said he loved me too? Risk my life to save him? I should kill him instead. Better idea: leave the Gestapo to torture and kill the bastard. And yet, here I was searching for him. Why? Because I knew this wasn't an escape just for him. It was a rehearsal of his plan to get Miriam and Regina out of the ghetto before the Nazis sealed

3

our fate.

There were no sounds. The starving residents of the ghetto, zombies, were in their own rat-holes. The Jewish Order Service, Chairman Rumkowski's police force, were not at their stations. It was past the Nazi-imposed curfew. Not even the thugs of the Chairman's, our authoritarian leader's, brutal police were allowed on the streets. Only fools and those wishing to commit suicide, and there were many, would dare venture out. Who would risk being arrested or shot by Nazi sentries who were using Jews for target practice? Singer. And now me. We were the fools.

Where would Singer go? I thought of his recent accounts of shooting incidents by the German sentries. I suspected he used his alleged hunt for "eye-witness" reports to hide clandestine liaisons with Miriam. How could he do this to me? Anger swelled inside me again. Go back home! You owe the little shit nothing! Let him try and escape! Let him get killed. But it was Singer, my coworker, my friend. He was an idiot, but I couldn't let him die. In the year since we began working together to document the daily events in the ghetto, he, the pesky gadfly, the wild-eyed, long-haired idealist, had wormed his way into my heart. It was a classic case of love and hate. Love for him and Miriam overcoming, at least for the present, my hate for what they did to me. "Zgierska Street!" Almost all of his attempted escape reports centered on the barriers along that demolished area. No wonder he volunteered to write up those shootings for our chronicle. "Damn him!" My tormented mind calculated the many opportunities he gave himself to be alone with Miriam while I, the naïve husband, worked in the Archives section of the Jewish Ghetto Administration. We, the other chroniclers, excused his absences as the natural restlessness of the young playboy, cooped up too long with older men, Julian Cukier, Oskar Rosenfeld, and me, recording the nightmare of suffering in our ghetto for our Chairman. How could we expect a young man, full of life, to become a bookkeeper of the dead and dying? That is what we had become as the Nazis deprived us of food, fuel and freedom and Rumkowski, their appointed Eldest of the Jews, our much-feared Chairman, planned concerts and holidays for his cohorts while tightening his hold on every aspect of our lives.

In the darkness, no street lamps, my black coat was perfect camouflage, but I was cautious, walking quickly, not running. Running attracted attention and bullets. I had my government identification in my hand and had rehearsed what to say if I were stopped by the police: "My friend was drinking rotten alcohol, celebrating the new year. He is young. He went insane. He is out here somewhere. Please help me find him?" Surely Jews, even the brutes of Chairman Rumkowski's police, would help other Jews against the Nazi sentries. "He's my infant daughter's godfather." I almost choked saying that. How could I have trusted him?

Miriam accused me of being blind to the greed and ruthlessness of Rumkowski, but I had to be. He was my employer, and many other residents, and I, believed he was the savior of the ghetto. If the Chairman was strict in enforcing German decrees; it was to prevent the Gestapo from having any possible excuse to take over. If the Nazis suspected he was weak, had any evidence of his loss of control over the factories supplying their military, the wolves would devour us as they were doing all of Europe. But Miriam was right, I'd been blind. I should have known from the first time I introduced her to Singer, when I saw her blush at his handsome face, that she was lost to me. I, scholarly in appearance and fifteen years her senior, could not compete with the adventurous charmer who kept his past a mystery. Tall, athletic, long, black hair, he was what a girl Miriam's age would swoon for. I, barely five foot nine, balding and cursed with poor eyesight and thick glasses, made a wholesome father-figure, but a lover? I'd fooled myself. Love had blinded me. No more.

Zgierska Street ran behind the boarded-up storefronts and tenement buildings that were over-run by rats and roaches. There were no alleyways. No place in which to duck and find safety. Where would Singer go? I was near the intersection he had mentioned so often, looking ahead for police, German, Jewish, and thieves who would kill for a crumb of bread or my government papers. What if he left hours ago? No. He said he would wait until just after midnight. It was New Year's Eve. The sentry, lonely, far away from his German home, would be drunk...might, if God willed it, be asleep. Humans all over the world get drunk on the turning of the year. German sentries are human." Are they? He said he'd seen the sentry in a stupor on Christmas Eve...that was Singer's brilliant escape plan.

A narrow gap between two vacant, boarded-up apartment houses. I squeezed in. What the hell was I doing out here?

I peered into the dark. Nothing moved. It was a trash-strewn alley, a suitable place for Singer to watch, wait, for the sentry to sleep. He wasn't here. The barbed wire looked silvery in the moonlight. I'd never been this close to the sentry booth at night. The cruel, sharp, barbs, clumps of wire that had torn into human flesh, sparkled like diamonds, like the metal sheen of thousands of tiny knives. I saw in my mind the body of a woman hanging from the wire, flesh torn by the barbs. Just hanging, arms outstretched, blood seeping down from her wounds. She was nearly over the top of the vicious fence. The woman's face...Miriam?

But Miriam was home, safe, while I was out hunting for her bastard of a lover. Who was insane? Me, or my unhappy wife, who begged me to find a way to escape this German corral for Jews? None of us understood why, in the heat of war, the Germans would devote valuable resources, men, money, and time on the mass relocation of Jews who they branded as undesirables. As our senior colleague, the kindly Dr. Rosenfeld often said, "Only the Germans know." Singer invariably added, "The Chairman knows." Did he? No time to debate that now.

The intersection ahead offered no cover. I checked from my concealed position, expecting to see an Order Service officer standing at his usual post on our side of the wall. Maybe they were celebrating in their barracks, or 'stupping' their wives in their flats. When was the

CHAPTER 1

last time I made love with Miriam? "Oh, God. Focus." The corners were deserted. "Where is that damn idiot? If the sentries don't kill him, I will."

I inched forward, to the west end of Zgierska. The sentry booth was a few hundred yards in front. Everything had been demolished to provide no hiding place near this guarded entry that separated our enclosed slum from the city of Lodz. I still could not see the end of the barbed wire, but I was getting too close to the booth. I had to stop, take a breath. Could I get closer without being at risk? I couldn't see if anyone was inside. So many had been killed here. I'm a father. My daughter, Regina, my new-born beautiful child, needs me. Hadn't I done everything anyone could to find Singer? I expected to see armed sentries leap from the booth their rifles firing at me with deafening blasts. I'm not Singer. And yet, I didn't leave.

I searched again, my eyes blurred with exhaustion and despair. If there had been a shape…standing, crouching, crawling, near the wire, I would have risked it. I saw nothing. I tried my best…tried to save Miriam's lover. I had to go back. And yet, the fence was close, so tempting. Singer may have been right, the damn sentry could be in a drunken stupor. I can escape… escape from everything. One way or the other, free or dead, the ordeal would be over. Would death be worse than this? Regina. I had no choice. I backed away, a frightened rat scuttling back into the shadows.

As I made my way home, the frigid air biting through my coat, my anger turned to numbness, something I could live with. I kept my eyes searching for Singer, but I was calm enough to realize finding him had been a long-shot. He knew the ghetto, its hidden pathways and sewers. He had connections in the black market. Those criminals could have helped him escape hours ago. I must have been blinded by emotion to risk this, I thought, as the stupidity of what I was doing sank in. At any step, I might be shot, and Regina would lose her father. Miriam would lose…what was I now to her?

I held my government identification as if a document that could be forged on the black market would shield me. I doubted it would do any good if the Nazis intercepted me. They shot Jews on sight. We had no value to them, not even those working in their service.

By the time I got to our dark street, I was soaked with sweat. I leaned against the wall of the building's entryway, calming myself, trying to recover from my fear and anger. Singer was wrong: two plus two always equals four. I could hear his voice criticizing my faith in logic and mathematics, but there wasn't any escaping that simple, universal, rule: two plus two must always equal four, or the entire structure of human existence collapses. Miriam must never suspect I know about her and Singer. "I'll hide the letter." I felt tears well in my eyes again but fought them back. *Yes, I loved the boy...still...in spite of everything. I'll hide what I know and pretend to be blind. For Regina, I'll pretend I never saw his damn letter.*

I was barely able to climb the three flights of stairs. The banister, wood, had been stolen for fuel for someone's heat. I cracked the door open. The sound of breathing told me Miriam was asleep. I was grateful for that small gift from God. I would not have to answer her questions. I would not have to add to my lies. My baby was breathing rhythmically in the crib. I could have watched her for hours, but I was drained.

Keeping my coat and shoes on, I left a puddle on the bare wood floors. I didn't bother wiping it up but fell into my chair. My last thoughts were of Singer. Where had he gone? I wished I'd found him. I had thought of beating him up for that letter, for his betrayal. I couldn't do that. I'm not a fighter. He would have pulverized me. Would he? In the letter, he said he loved me. He said that was why he was leaving. "I can't bear to hurt you."

Afraid of having nightmares, I fought to keep my eyes open. I told myself it was Singer's fault, not Miriam's. How could she resist him? Even I, who should have hated him, couldn't stop worrying, caring. My inner voice refused to let me have peace: "He's an idiot! Not evil. Hitler is evil. Rumkowski? I don't know if he is or not. Oscar Singer is not. If Miriam loves him, I'll step aside. If she wants him...so be it. If he is alive...if he is here...if...if...if." How could I sleep with Singer unaccounted for? How could I pretend nothing had changed? God, I hated Miriam's face. I couldn't look in her lying hazel eyes. Who was I kidding? I still loved her. I loved them both. That was the curse with which I was now condemned to live.

CHAPTER 2

J ANUARY 2, 1942
A rumor concerning the resettlement of the entire population spread through the ghetto like wildfire. It was even announced that the Registry Office would be supplying the authorities (German) with the relevant data in the next few hours.

Singer's letter was burning a hole in my coat as I trudged the muddy roads to the Jewish Ghetto Administration building more than a mile away. I pretended for Miriam that the note did not exist. I rehearsed in my brain options on how I'd confront Singer when he showed up in our workroom. I did not want to embarrass him or myself before the others. That fool would never try anything so dangerous as an escape, I told myself. I could have been killed while he was in bed with one of his lady friends. I tried not to let rage boil inside me, but small reminders were unpredictable triggers. When Miriam bent her head so I could kiss her forehead, and not her lips, I could not stop thinking those lips had touched Singer's treacherous mouth. I saw his gloating smile. When I saw her breasts outlined by her filthy chemise, I thought of Singer's hands and mouth on their flesh. I had no idea how long their affair had been going on, but it explained so much. The evidence was undeniable. Two plus two. So I did not try to deny, only to live with it as one lives with a shadow. But I would make Singer aware that I knew. *He will have to stop. I will give him some excuse to provide Miriam, but it has to stop.*

"It's a new year," Dr. Rosenfeld said, letting out a deep sigh which misted in the unheated air. "Sad to say, nothing has changed."

I had to agree, although the rumors of the emptying of our ghetto had put everyone on edge since no one ever heard where the deportees were sent. When Julian Cukier entered, fresh from a meeting with Neftalin, Rumkowski's trusted Deputy, I met him head-on. "Are the resettlement rumors true?"

"Of course, not. The Chairman himself delivered a public address in the most vigorous terms, addressing these rumors." He picked up a note Neftalin had given him and read the last sentence aloud, "Such an authoritative denial of the panicky reports caused the populace to regain its calm at once." You see, the Chairman has calmed the situation as he always does. You must have more confidence in our great leader."

I expected Singer to burst into his usual cynical laughter at such an optimistic generalization of the ghetto's mood, but he wasn't here. There was nobody to question this propaganda. "You're really going to put that in our reports?" I asked, surprised how much I'd been influenced by Singer.

Cukier looked surprised. "Engineer, are you questioning me?"

"No." What would be the point? Cukier was the Chairman's man, the appointed leader of our small crew.

Rosenfeld shook his head. "The gypsy camp is no more," he said after reading a report from the Housing Department. "That's a blessing."

"It was a hotbed of disease anyway," Cukier remarked. "More than 400 died there in December alone."

"400 in one month?" The number was notable even in our circumstances where death had become commonplace.

Rosenfeld laughed bitterly. "Always the numbers with you. Numbers mean nothing to most people, my dear Engineer. I will tell you what means something. They are taking the bodies, as many as they can fit, and throwing them into newly constructed wagons. Have you seen them? They are dragged by emaciated horses twice daily through our streets, collecting indistinguishable bodies piled one on another…" The professor, the oldest member of our small crew, chewed thoughtfully on the stem of his empty pipe.

Cukier grimaced. "Well, it's necessary, but not much longer. For the last ten days, the gypsies have been taken away in trucks. The camp is deserted now."

"This was ordered to stop the spread of the disease?" I asked.

Cukier nodded. "It was judged the best way to stop the spread of typhus to the rest of us."

"Where did they send them?" I asked, reading the memo. "Does anyone know?"

Cukier didn't respond.

"Only the Germans know," Rosenfeld said.

I heard Singer add, "And someone else." What was wrong with me? Why did the voice in my head sound like that fool? Late as usual, I thought, wondering if his lateness hid his trysts with Miriam. I had to stop thinking of them, but how?

"Did you know there is no longer any mail in or out of the ghetto?" Cukier asked. "Another order from the German authorities."

"I wonder why they did that now?" I asked.

"Only the Germans know," Rosenfeld said again.

"Singer's late," Cukier grumbled. "I should fire the pain-in-the-ass."

I felt a chill rush down my spine. I hoped it didn't show.

"He's probably sleeping off a night with some whore," Cukier said. "He's never grown up." He laughed. "I envy him."

Rosenfeld looked angry. "He's a good boy. He always brings us good eyewitness stories and interviews. I don't blame him for not wanting to be cooped-up here so many hours every day with a bunch of grumbling old men."

I shivered when he spoke about the "eyewitness stories." I knew the truth behind Singer's lies. He probably had confederates who supplied him his so-called reports while he was with my wife. The sly bastard.

Cukier smiled. "Since you like the rascal, Professor, okay, I won't fire him. But I think we need more help. The paperwork here is mounting." He pulled out a memo from the Order Service. "There's been another death at the Police Station."

I froze. The Police Station was a euphemism for the Gestapo. Was the victim Singer? I closed my eyes, praying again to the God, who I no longer believed in, who no longer listened to Jewish pleas, that it wasn't Oscar.

"According to the report, the cause of death was a cardiac defect," Cukier said. "The man was young though."

A young man…a heart attack? The Germans pulled any excuse they could find. "What's the man's name?" I asked, gripping the table, afraid to hear Singer's name.

"No name is included." Cukier scoured the report. "It says the deceased's brother, the director of one of the food distribution points, is also under arrest."

I breathed a sigh of relief. To my knowledge, Singer did not have a brother. Miriam, Regina, and I were his only family. It occurred to me that I'd never asked about his family. Why didn't I ask? Why didn't I know anything about these men I called my coworkers…friends. Were they friends? Singer was always tight-lipped about his past. I let it go because I was amused by his youthful nature, his playboy image. Was it a façade? Did he have other secrets? Did we all have secrets?

Rosenfeld eyed me curiously. "You look worried? Are you alright?"

"Miriam wasn't well last night. That's all."

"I'm sorry. That is normal after giving birth, especially under this kind of stress. Wish your sweet wife better from me," Rosenfeld said, still eyeing me with that curious look.

"Listen to this," Cukier interrupted. "We're all trying to get out of the ghetto, and this guy was trying to get in. Apparently, he's a Christian and in love with a Jewess who was transported here from Prague."

"Love makes us do strange things," Rosenfeld said.

I know all about that, I thought. "So, what did this idiot do because of love?" I asked, thinking of another idiot who I felt like killing.

Now Cukier looked curiously at me. "According to his girlfriend, he set out on the long journey from Prague to Lodz on foot. He then slipped in successfully through the barbed wire—"

"How did he do that?" I thought of Singer. If a man from Prague, love-struck enough to walk to this hell-hole, could get through the barricade, then Singer might have escaped. Here was a ray of hope he might help us...help Miriam and Regina.

"It doesn't say, but he got caught by Order Service police who turned him over to the German criminal police," Cukier said, shaking his head.

"Oh shit," Rosenfeld muttered. "Jews turning someone over to the Nazis...a sin...a damn sin."

"They have to. It's by accordance with the ruling on combatting illegal entries into the ghetto," Cukier said and coughed into his handkerchief.

"Which the Chairman signed," I remarked, again taking Singer's role of resident skeptic.

Rosenfeld wagged his pipe at Cukier. "Not in my day. No Jew would ever betray another brother or sister. It's a sin. Who knows what the Germans will do to him?"

"What happened to the man?" I asked, grateful it wasn't Singer.

Cukier read lower. "It says his fate is unknown."

"Nobody knows?" I asked.

"The Germans know," Rosenfeld replied.

I wondered if the Germans knew where Singer was.

CHAPTER 3

J ANUARY 5, 1942: *DEATH OF AN ORDER SERVICE PRISONER*
On January 4, at 5:00 P.M. a man who had been a prisoner died
while at Precinct II of the Order Service. He was due to be released
soon.

Was it my imagination or had Miriam become withdrawn? She looked
as if she wanted to ask me a question, but never did. I suspected what
it was. It was the same question dominating my mind every time an
arrest or death report fell into our growing pile from the Jewish police
administration. My anger at Oscar's and Miriam's betrayal was still
simmering, but I was more concerned about Singer's failure to return.
I was helpless, not knowing what to do. I could not talk to Miriam
about what I feared. Each day I prayed for some answer, and each
day, I prayed that answer would not come in one of the routine police
department announcements of more deaths. I could not suffer the
pain to add Regina's godfather's name, my friend, to the long list of
martyrs dying senselessly in the wasteland that was our ghetto. God,
do not add this to my torment, was my daily prayer.

Miriam gave no sign she missed my affection. She spent much
of the time cuddling Regina, cooing at her, teasing her with fingers
weathered by the cold of winter without heat. I had gotten to the
point where I no longer missed her affection either. The baby was
all that kept us together, our fragile common bond. I could watch
her antics for hours. I understood why Singer had fallen in love with
her. The feel of her softness, her vulnerability, against my chest was

the best moment of the day. It also was the only time I missed the warmth of Miriam's head against my shoulder, her hair, now matted and unkempt, had been feather-soft against my cheek. But that was long ago. It was in another dream…another life.

Work became my escape, but there was no escape from our reality. Every day brought another shitload of tragedies that were becoming a blur to us. We searched for anything that could break the monotony, even if it was horrific. I thought little could still disturb me, but I should have known better.

"This is Dr. Bernard Heilig," Cukier announced. "He is an outstanding scholar, an expert in economics and political thinking."

He's young. Another damn Singer? But he did not have the looks of a playboy, but more of a battered scarecrow, a narrow, beardless, face with a sallow, pock-marked complexion. His eyes looked vacant through his thick eyeglasses.

"I've heard of your work," Dr. Rosenfeld said. "I'm surprised you are so young."

Heilig didn't answer.

"Dr. Heilig was deported from Prague," Cukier said. "He lost track of his entire family."

As did we all, I thought, wondering if I'd ever find out what happened to Miriam's parents. We left them in Lublin after I found employment in Lodz. I thought working for a Polish firm would secure our safety. Another time I'd fooled myself. Even Cukier's father, a respected Lodz factory owner, wasn't spared. God knows where they all are now, I thought, staring at Heilig. His haggard appearance and nervous demeanor made me uneasy. He looked as if he was trembling. I wondered why such a timid man had been selected to help us. The Chairman said our work was important to let the future know about Jewish culture now threatened by Hitler. He called our work, "a message in the bottle" that might be the only evidence that survives. He warned us that our punishment would be severe if the authorities, our euphemism for the German Ghetto Authority, discovered what we were doing in the building we shared with them. I'd accepted the risk for Miriam's sake. I needed the job to provide food for her, so I agreed to work for the leader of the ghetto though many called him the devil. Had this newcomer understood the danger? As I studied his nervous mannerisms, I was afraid he would be easily broken by the Gestapo if they got wind of our work. This Heilig may have been young like Singer, but something wasn't right about him. He would be our weak link, something we couldn't afford.

Cukier's eyes were on me when he said, "I sent Dr. Heilig to hear the Chairman's New Year's Speech as his first assignment. Will you please share your report?"

Heilig's voice was almost inaudible as he began to recite the Chairman's speech without any notes.

I was falling asleep, not having slept the night before when Cukier said, "Remarkable. Isn't it? Dr. Heilig is not only a gifted writer but has a photographic memory."

I was good with numbers, but a photographic memory? This I had to see.

"Doctor...Bernard, would you mind providing the main points in the Chairman's own words?"

"He can do that without any notes in front of him?" I interrupted, doubting anyone had such ability.

"Just listen," Cukier said, looking proud of his latest acquisition.

Rosenfeld leaned forward, sucking on his empty pipe.

Heilig turned skittish eyes on Cukier and said, "Chairman M.C. Rumkowski began by reviewing events of the past year. I quote, "I don't know what interests my esteemed audience more, the past, the future, or just plain gossip.""

"He said exactly that?" I asked.

Heilig didn't even nod his head, but continued in his monotone, "He then said, "When I cast my mind back I am first filled with pride by the record speed at which the ghetto was turned into a place of work. We have an army of close to 50,000 people employed. Such a large number of workers has to be treated seriously by everyone, including, first and foremost, those who make policy."

"We know who that is," Rosenfeld said.

Echoes of Singer? Where was that sonofabitch?

Heilig continued as if no one existed in our room. "From the beginning, I have been striving to achieve one basic goal...to demonstrate to the authorities that the ghetto is composed exclusively of working people."

"Those sound like his words. Amazing," Rosenfeld said.

"I never forget anything anyone says." Heilig snorted and then continued his remarkable rendition, "The Chairman went on to say, 'Unfortunately, at times, people have ridiculed my intentions.'" He stopped reciting. "Do you want to hear more?"

I was still skeptical. Was it an act of some kind? Was this Heilig a fake, like the mind-readers in a circus?

Cukier said, "Please go on? He is our esteemed leader and deserves to be heard with his words intact." He smiled at me. "None of us can emulate this young man's feat."

Heilig shrugged as if accustomed to such compliments. "Your Chairman went on to say, 'The difficult task of correcting the evils caused by that lack of understanding on the part of the public now awaits me.'"

""Correcting the evils" sounds like a threat." Oh, no. Was I becoming another Singer?

Cukier snapped, "Could you save your comments? These are our Chairman's exact words."

Heilig continued, sounding more confident. "The Chairman next called the profiteers and black market smugglers 'hyenas.'"

"Good. They undermine his efforts," Rosenfeld said.

Singer would have laughed at that. Those thieves were his best friends.

Heilig raised his eyes to the ceiling and with his memory apparently refreshed, began again. "Your Chairman then claimed many of your immigrants are 'parasites' trying to exploit everyone else and expecting to live on welfare."

"Very true," Cukier remarked. "The Chairman has his finger on the pulse of the ghetto."

"More like his fist around its throat," I heard Singer and Miriam in my mind.

Heilig droned on, "He condemned those that hide valuable possessions and demanded they turn them over or face severe punishments."

"The Germans have already confiscated all our furs, cameras, bicycles, musical instruments and jewelry. Do they want my gloves too?" Rosenfeld hid his gloves in his coat pocket.

"Those are safe for now," I said, remembering how the gloves I'd stolen for him from a dead body, had subsequently been stolen from him. His hands had been so cold until Singer had given him a new pair of gloves. Singer and his connections. "Even the Germans don't want your hands to be frozen by this blasted winter, dear Professor."

Rosenfeld didn't laugh. He put the gloves back on his always cold hands.

Heilig didn't laugh either. "The Chairman then affirmed his goal of creating jobs for everyone in the ghetto. He called work the 'passport' and said he was going to make 'big changes' to 'help assure everyone was pulling their weight.'"

"It's as I've said numerous times," Cukier interjected. "The Eldest of the Jews, our Chairman, has the only plan that can save us."

With Singer absent, there was no one to argue. Heilig was a recording device, no soul, no heart. He was not a Singer. Neither was I.

Heilig, as if in a trance, continued, "The Chairman launched into an attack on gossip. I quote, 'Perhaps the authors of those panic-producing stories are even lurking about here, in this audience. I would like to murder them.'"

Cukier looked stunned. "Heilig, those were his exact words?"

"Of course. I never have to make up words. Your Chairman was emphatic. I'd say he lost his temper. He said, 'I would like to murder them.'"

I could believe the Chairman would want to murder the rumor mongers. He often claimed they were spreading fear and depression undermining the wellbeing of the ghetto and threatening the productivity of his factories. He, and his family, owned every factory, department, and public kitchen in the ghetto, which is why some claimed they were becoming rich on the sweat of their slaves.

Cukier looked dubious, but said, "Continue, please?"

"Did he address the relocations?" I interrupted.

Cukier frowned, but said, "You may answer."

"Chairman Rumkowski addressed that next, saying, 'At the present time, only those who are, in my opinion, deserving of such a fate will be resettled elsewhere.'"

Another threat, I thought but kept my mouth shut. While I believed Rosenfeld and Cukier would not report me, I had trusted Singer too. Look where that got me. One word from Cukier and I could be placed on the resettlement list. It was not that I loved the ghetto, but nobody knew where our resettled citizens were being taken. The Germans promised improved conditions and plentiful food in northern farm areas. Starving as we were, I did not blame anyone for wanting out of the ghetto but wondered why we had not heard news of those that had left on previous resettlement actions. "The devil you know is better than the devil you don't."

Heilig abruptly spat, "He is now God and jury—"

"What did you say?" Cukier leaped out of his seat.

Heilig jumped to attention, his hands at his sides, terror in his face. He was trembling.

Cukier's eyes were fiery. "Repeat what you said. That's an order."

Heilig mumbled, "I'm sorry. I'm sorry."

What kind of man had they saddled us with? Singer was problematic enough, but this coward sniveling in front of us? He was neurotic, a mess. Yes, he had a good memory, but was that reason enough to endanger all of our lives with this lunatic?

Cukier repeated, "Tell me what you said. Now."

Heilig stared at his shoes. "I was wrong to say that. It slipped out. It won't happen again."

Cukier replied coldly. "We do not offer our personal opinions here." He bit his lip. "You're new. You'll soon learn that we keep our personal politics to ourselves. Our task is to report events objectively, as the Chairman, the Eldest of the Jews, has employed us to do. It is our directive to support our administration at all times."

I heard Singer giggling. How often he protested our unquestioning support of the Chairman's policies and actions. "But he is our employer, our benefactor. We owe Rumkowski our survival," we'd argue in vain. Singer would stare at us with contempt and reply, "You're writing propaganda. Rumkowski is wrong. We should be fighting the Nazis, not cozying up to the Jew-haters who want to destroy us."

Cukier coughed into his nose rag. "Continue, but no more personal comments. Do you understand?" He coughed again.

Heilig nodded. "Our great leader." He looked at Cukier for approval, "went on to say, 'The authorities are full of admiration for the work which has been performed here, and it is due to that work that they have confidence in me. Their approval of my motion to reduce the number of deportees from 20,000 to 10,000 is a sign of that confidence.'"

Oh, God! The rumors were true. The Chairman confirmed them. 10,000 to be deported? Rumkowski said it was half of what the Nazis requested. But we're still deporting our citizens! I wondered who was playing the numbers game now. Whatever the number, he had confirmed the rumors. Ten thousand more Jews were being removed from the ghetto, and nobody knew where they were going.

Cukier, looking disturbed, asked, "Is there more?"

"Yes, sir. To combat gossip, the Chairman said he is going to create..." Heilig glanced at the ceiling again and then said, "'Special confidential agents.' Those were his exact words. Oh yes, he added the following statement: 'Bear in mind that at the center of all my projects is the aspiration that honest people may sleep in peace. Nothing bad will happen to people of good will.'" Heilig let out a tight-lipped smile. "Those were his exact words."

Cukier coughed and then stared at his handkerchief. "How did the audience take that last bit?"

"There was thunderous applause."

Applause at a veiled threat? This speech would have killed Singer. I could imagine Miriam's reaction if she got hold of the transcript. Thunderous applause? Perhaps from the elite few, government officials, factory managers, his family members, who lived far better than the masses.

"Your memory is astonishing," Cukier said, then burst into coughing again.

I saw scattered light red stains on the nose rag. Were they old or new?

Heilig was speaking more confidently, perhaps responding to our leader's compliment. "The Chairman also spoke of the recent labor strikes and said, 'Had the strike attempts that took place here recently come to the attention of the authorities, the snow would have been red with blood.'"

Singer had said the snow was red with blood from the Jewish police using clubs on their fellow Jews during the strike in the Chairman's factories. The news that Jews, even police, had bloodied the snow with the blood of our brethren, had been a shock. Miriam and Singer had become furious. Miriam and Singer...every thought, any mention, of their names, resurrected the clues I'd been too blind to see. The change in Miriam, her outspoken anger at our Chairman's actions, questioning his policies, now made sense. I'd been amused at first by her unprecedented interest in ghetto politics. Later, I found it annoying. Singer had been annoying...

"Don't you agree, Engineer, Rumkowski is right? All the authorities are waiting for is an excuse to take over if our administration loses control." Cukier wagged his finger at Heilig. "Why can't everyone see that? Only if the authorities believe we are essential to their war effort will they leave us alone."

I nodded, numbed by everything, unable to focus. I felt as if I wasn't here. I was out of my body, staring down at the hopeless, blind, fool I'd become.

Heilig replied. "The Chairman addressed that: 'Remember, comrades and friends that day and night, my mind is concerned with improving the situation in the ghetto, and I am near the breaking point from constant exertion.'"

"Poor baby." I searched for Singer, but the words had been my own silent response.

Cukier exclaimed, "Did I not tell you his memory is astounding?"

I was impressed, a bit jealous.

Heilig gave a weak smile. "The big thing he repeated at several points was 'the plan for the New Year is work, work, and more work!' Is that a slogan of sorts?"

I bit my tongue, hearing Singer's laughter at the familiar exhortation to work. It was at the heart of Rumkowski's grand strategy: turn the ghetto into an industrial hub for the Reich to prove they couldn't live without us. "Collaborating with killers and Jew-haters won't save us." I could hear Singer's shrill voice echoing in my brain.

Heilig was still holding the floor. "The Chairman ended with a plea: 'I am doing everything possible. I should not be required to do what lies beyond the bounds of the possible. Brothers and sisters, without your help I cannot achieve anything. But with your help, I am certain that I will succeed in carrying out my mission to create conditions that allow us to live through the current period in good health, and to preserve the lives and the health of the people of the ghetto society and its young generation.'"[1]

Heilig shrank in stature with his recitation completed. I thought he looked as if ready to collapse, a boneless deflated bag of wind now that he'd run out of someone else's words. He was an actor without a role, with no words or personality of his own.

Cukier rose to his feet and extended his hand to Heilig. "Now I know why Neftalin selected you. You are an amazing asset to our mission of preserving the history of what may well be the last great Jewish community in Poland. Mazel tov and welcome."

For a second, I thought Cukier was going to give our barely human recorder a 'thunderous applause' or a kiss on the cheek. I'd never Julian, a bachelor, with a woman, I abruptly thought. How little I knew of these men.

Heilig eyed Cukier's hand for several seconds and then extended his hand. It shook slightly. There were bruises on top of his palm, and a finger looked crooked. Broken?

"You did a fine job. Welcome to the team," Cukier continued, pumping the younger man's hand as if he were a politician stumping for votes.

Rosenfeld gave Heilig a nod. "He's not a Singer," he whispered to me, holding up his gloved hands.

I hope not, I thought, as I wondered why our newest member aroused my suspicions. Was it resentment? Jealousy? I didn't have much time to think. Cukier told Heilig to write up his report and directed me to type it up after it was written. "I like the Chairman's speech, especially the last sentences. Let's add, 'The speech produced a great impression on the audience.' Do you agree?" He aimed his eyes at Heilig.

Heilig gave him a hint of a smile.

---

[1] *This chapter contains some phrases from Chairman Rumkowski's actual New Year speech. Rather than paraphrasing them, I felt they should be included as intact as possible to provide a glimpse at the Chairman's attitudes and policies as expressed in his own words and recorded in The Chronicle of the Lodz Ghetto and other sources.*

The Weasel worried me. He was hiding something, but I had other things to think about. I wondered if the others heard what I'd caught in the speech, "Nothing bad will happen to people of good will." It was a veiled threat of impending harm to those who did not share the Chairman's policies. Was I still one of the "people of good will?" I wished Singer would show up so I could find myself again. Arguing with our radical invariably steered me toward defending our Chairman. Without Singer, I was meandering toward the opposition. Was that why Heilig was studying me with his slits of eyes? Weasel. Good nickname. Great memory or not, I didn't trust the Weasel. I didn't trust anyone anymore, not even Miriam.

CHAPTER 4

J ANUARY 13, 1942: DEATHS AND BIRTHS
  *In the course of four days, 216 people died in the ghetto. There were
  births only on the 13th of January—three to be precise (two boys and
one girl). The principal causes of death were...*

"Do you realize that our mortality rate has risen to an average of 46
deaths per day?" I interrupted Heilig's reading of the daily police
report. I had given him the nickname of, 'Weasel,' because of his lean
and nervous appearance and my distrust.

Cukier looked up from his pile of reports from the Chairman's
numerous departments. "Let him finish. What are the major causes
of death? I'd like to know."

"Exhaustion, tuberculosis, and heart disease."

Damn ghoul, I thought. I looked to Cukier for his reaction. There
was none visible, but I saw blood stains on his handkerchief. I saw
them, yet could not weep. We were surrounded by the sick and dying.
"Exhaustion?" It was a euphemism for starving, freezing, deprivation,
all caused by the Nazi hatred of Jews.

Rosenfeld, looking incredibly bony, his voice more of a croak than
ever. "At least there is some control of the typhus."

I could hear Singer's voice crying out in anger, "There are no gypsies
here anymore! They're all gone! Where did they take all those poor
souls? God only knows." And Rosenfeld, as had become his habit,
would reply, "The Germans know." Then Singer would stick the
needle into all of us and add, "The Eldest of the Jews also knows."

Did he? Nobody could know exactly what the Chairman knew. His speeches had become tirades and threats at anyone who, for whatever reason, undermined his authority. His police were everywhere, enforcing his commands, targeting anyone who in any way obstructed the smooth operation of his factories and departments. The threat of expulsion hung over us like a death sheet. While existence in the ghetto was one of starvation, freezing cold, increasing numbers of barely-alive zombies and uncollected corpses, nobody wanted to be selected for the deportations, destination unknown.

Even Miriam, who hated the ghetto, asked, "Do you think we are in danger of being deported? Immigrants are the first he selects." She was holding Regina close to her breast.

My child's eyes lit up when she saw me. That was enough to calm my thoughts, my too vivid images of Miriam with Singer. God, I hated him, but I missed the pest. I wished she would ask me about him so I could tell her that I knew their secret. She never did. If she thought of her lover at all, it was in the unreachable silence of her mind. I was aloof, but still felt compelled to reassure and protect her. Her parents had placed their trust in me. "No, Miriam, we are not going to be selected."

"Because of your job?" She held Regina tighter, her hand cradling my child's head.

She never asked about my work. If I was Rumkowski's executioner, she did not want to know. I'd been warned the first day, by the Chairman, that revealing what I was doing, a task banned by the Germans would endanger her, so I avoided discussing it. There were walls of secrets between us, and I no longer wanted to try to scale them. "Yes, because of my job."

"So, we are safe?"

"We are safe."

The safest I felt was when I was buried in my work in the Administration building, even though it was also the headquarters of the German Ghetto Authority. That was why there were no longer protesters by the front doors. The Jewish police, under Rumkowski's firm hand, had evolved into a strong defense force, shielding we administrators from the residents, the zombies. The only vehicles were the German motorcars and the Chairman's horse-driven coach, usually parked in front of our building, a brass plate identifying its owner. The conspicuous plaque was needless. No other horse or coach was allowed within our community, except the hearses. They also needed no identification.

Heilig's voice interrupted my thoughts. "We missed this proclamation," he said.

I lifted my head from my arms. "Another proclamation?" He handed it to me, and I read it for Julian:

JANUARY 9, 1942

BOOTS MUST BE TURNED IN

Proclamation No. 350 was posted and, by order of the authorities, ski and mountain boots in sizes 40 and up should be presented for sale at the Bank of the Eldest of the Jews...In the event that boots are discovered after the above-mentioned deadline, they will be confiscated, and their owners will incur the appropriate penalties...

"We're fortunate they leave us our underwear," I mumbled, realizing I sounded remarkably like my missing friend. I noticed Rosenfeld remove his gloves and shove them into his coat pocket. "Don't worry, your gloves are still safe."

He looked uncertain but put them back on. "Nothing is safe anymore. I miss my pipe. I would even pay Singer to find tobacco for me."

He meant on the black market. There was no tobacco in the ghetto. The sole distribution point was selling cigarettes rolled from leaves of an unknown origin. The Chairman had to send police to break up a riot in front of the smoke shop and then issued orders that all smokers be registered so the fake cigarettes could be distributed equitably. Meanwhile, he was always seen with cigarettes in his mouth. It was, he said, his only vice. "I don't smoke," I said, thinking ruefully that I would pay Singer, or anyone else, to find Singer for me.

"I no longer smoke either," Rosenfeld replied tapping his empty pipe on our table. "It might kill me."

Heilig looked confused.

I could not warm up to him. I sifted through my pile of memos. "It's begun," I exclaimed, reading the headline from the special commission for resettlement. "The resettlement is happening."

Everyone shot their eyes at me.

I could barely hold the paper still. "The office sent out two thousand warrants for expulsion to prisoners and their families, newcomers, prostitutes, and other "undesirable elements.""

"He warned them over and over," Cukier remarked.

I wondered if Cukier believed in what he was saying. His face was covered with his handkerchief so I could not see his expression.

Heilig muttered. "That phrase, "undesirable elements," sounds too familiar."

He was subtler than Singer, but I knew what he meant: the Germans called all Jews, "undesirable elements." I'd caught that phrase too. It sent a chill through me.

Cukier replied, "Well, someone has to go. It is best that the enemies of our survival are the ones to leave." He burst into a terrible fit of coughing. "Someone must pick—"

"Why must they?"

I was surprised. It was Rosenfeld who said this.

"What do you mean?" Cukier stammered between coughs. "If we don't do it, the Nazis will. It will be worse for us…the law-abiding, the workers, the true citizens of Lodz—"

"Let them pick. Why are we doing their dirty work for them?" Rosenfeld's eyes were hard as stone. "My God, I have sat here meekly accepting for over a year. Silence condone. Singer, I miss him. He was obstinate, a cynic, but he was right. Jews do not sit quietly while other Jews are selected to go God knows where. My young friend—he

29

gave me more than my gloves—I'm afraid he was right all along."

Cukier shot back, "No. He was totally wrong. If our Eldest of the Jews had not taken control, our fate would have been sealed long ago. Rumkowski has single-handedly saved us from whatever hell Hitler has in store for Jews. Why should we risk the Germans selecting our best minds, our intelligentsia, our essential officials, when we can rid ourselves of the parasites that threaten our existence?"

"You mean the "undesirable elements?" Is that what you mean?" Rosenfeld asked, his wise eyes searching our leader's gaunt face.

"Yes," Cukier said so softly that I knew it was without conviction. "Yes, it is our survival that must be paramount." He gazed at his nose rag and sighed.

We didn't respond.

"Shall I read the rest?" Heilig asked.

Cukier nodded from behind his handkerchief.

The Weasel read without emotion, "The first transports will leave the ghetto on January 16th. Each transport will take 700 people per day. Those being resettled will be allowed 12.5 kilograms of luggage."

"That is not very much luggage," I commented.

"The numbers man strikes again," Rosenfeld remarked, casting me a sad smile.

Heilig looked at me and continued, "If the deportees do not appear at the appointed time, they will be forcibly conducted to the assembly point, and lose the right to take luggage with them."

"And so, it begins," Rosenfeld said.

Cukier broke the thick silence. "It is not all gloom and doom. On January 4th, the Chairman—we know how much he loves children—and a number of our highest officials attended the gala graduation ceremonies at the House of Culture of 85 graduating students from his Lyceum. I was there. It was wonderful to hear the graduates express their gratitude to the Chairman for being able to receive their diplomas." He turned to me. "Someday, your Regina will be a beneficiary of our Chairman's ardent love and devotion to children."

"Please, don't rush her growing up," I said, unwilling to face my child growing older when she had just been born, a miracle in our deprived conditions.

The others laughed.

I laughed too. We were desperate to find anything to break up the darkness.

"I'll write it up," Rosenfeld offered, removing a glove to receive the report.

"Be sure to emphasize how much the Chairman has done for our children," Cukier instructed. "Even Singer would not deny that." His eye wandered to the door. "I miss that scoundrel too."

That left us all with the unspoken question none of us wanted to ask aloud. Where was our young gadfly?

CHAPTER 5

J ANUARY 14-31, 1942: *200 bodies*
Because of the record increase in the mortality rate, over 200
unburied bodies had accumulated by the end of January in the
cemetery mortuary. They remain unidentified...

I immediately thought of Singer being among the 200 unidentified
bodies but told myself he would be outspoken even as one of the
unnamed dead. Our long-haired radical would stick out with his
insolent smirk and boyish charm. "Hello, ladies, I'm Oscar." Oh, God,
how could I think of him that way? It was difficult to concentrate.
Heilig was reading the endless stream of entries in his monotonous
voice.

The damn Weasel had no emotions, no soul. He recited the list of
tragic events as if reading a phone book, finally hitting on an entry that
caught my attention. "On January 19, the authorities announced the
'legal' shooting of Dr. Ulrich Schulz, who was shipped to the ghetto
from Prague. From the time of his arrival, he had been in Central
Prison on Czarniecki Steet."

I interrupted. "Why is this shooting a 'legal' shooting? What makes
this one different from a so-called 'illegal' shooting?"

"I don't know," Heilig replied, shrugging his narrow shoulders. "Is
there such a thing as a legal killing?"

Cukier replied, "I guess that the doctor violated one of the rules of
the German authorities. What does the report state?"

Rosenfeld searched our files. "Dr. Ulrich Schulz? Yes, apparently, on his way from Prague to the ghetto, he had "flown into a rage and slandered the police officials—Germans –who were on the train as escorts." He shook his head. "The doctor was a lawyer it says. He would have known better."

"My god!" It escaped my lips. "They killed a man because he allegedly 'slandered' some German officers?"

Rosenfeld nodded. "It says here that the Commandant of the Order Service was present at the shooting."

"There must be something more to this," Cukier said. "Not even the Germans would shoot someone dead for merely insulting some policemen. Our Chairman would never allow such a punishment for such a minor infraction."

"It says the Commandant was a witness to the execution," Rosenfeld said. "Just when you think you've hit bottom, there's a new low."

"I tell you there's something more here," Cukier protested. "No civilized people would execute someone for mere insults." He burst into a fit of coughing.

"Maybe he was one of the 'undesirable elements,'" Rosenfeld said.

Cukier turned toward him, fury in his eyes. He must have realized it was the mild-mannered old professor who had said this because he clammed up and turned away without launching a rebuke. "Let us turn to something else," he muttered.

"There's the matter of the deportations," I reminded him.

"Resettlement," Cukier corrected, using the accepted euphemism.

"It's been going on all month. The orders were mailed to prisoners and the others. I deliberately avoided the term, "undesirables" to avoid reigniting our leader's anger. Whole families were ordered to go to the assembly point at 7 Szklana Street. There, from 9 in the morning until 9 at night, registrations were conducted by teachers and other officials hurriedly appointed for the massive job." I paused to read a short note. "I have a note here from the commission that on the first day less than 500 of the 1000 selected showed up at the station." I looked at the others. "It goes on to say the deportees were brought in 'forcibly,' most during the night." Is this latter true? 'Forcibly?'"

Cukier was silent, his handkerchief ready in his hand.

Rosenfeld said, "Rumors are flying that these poor people are being taken to even colder climates where they must farm for themselves to survive." He rubbed his gloved hands together. "Imagine a place colder than this."

Heilig raised his hand to be recognized, another annoying habit. "I have a note that may be relevant. It says the deportees are given free items while waiting for transport." Heilig searched his note. "It says they are kept two to three days. In a school and vacant buildings. Oh, they get to exchange their ghetto money for German marks."

Cukier said, "That is a good sign. They will need those bills once they are resettled."

Until the information about the exchange of currency, did our leader also have doubts about our deportees' fate? I agreed this was hopeful since the need to convert money indicated the deportees would be relocated to areas where there were businesses. It helped ease our fears founded on rumors, and the fact that nobody heard from any of our resettled people again. These unfounded suspicions were now laid at rest. After all, why give people money if they would never have any use for it? This new evidence convinced us that all the disturbing insinuations about the tragic fate of our deportees were not credible. I would happily relay this bit of good news to Miriam.

Heilig smiled. "Here's more good news. The deportees also receive free food and clothing."

"Yes, that is hopeful too," I replied, breathing a sigh of relief.

"It is indeed," Heilig said with rare emotion. "It says they were given twelve thousand pairs of warm underwear, earmuffs, gloves, stockings, socks, and clogs."

"I could use new gloves and warm underwear now," Rosenfeld said, rubbing his gloved hands together. "Warm underwear is more valuable than gold in this weather."

We all laughed at that.

The laughter stopped when Heilig read, "The trains are made up of approximately 20 passenger cars, each holding 55 people."

"55 per car sounds comfortable enough," I said.

"The numbers man as always," Cukier laughed but then burst into coughing.

We were all working quietly when the door opened.

Germans? I jumped from my seat.

Neftalin's face told us more than words that something terrible had happened.

I prayed again that it wasn't news about Singer.

CHAPTER 6

J ANUARY 31, 1942: THE RESETTLEMENT ACTION IN
JANUARY
*Resettlement occurred in January from the 16th to the 29th and
included 14 transports. All told, 10,003 persons left the ghetto—4,853 men
and 5,750 women.*

Neftalin entered the room and ushered in a stocky man in a worn
coat. "This is Mr. Gustaf Hahn, the honorable Chairman of the Jewish
Council of Kalisz. The Chairman wishes you to extend him every
courtesy. He has much that he has already shared with us, but the
Chairman wants to be certain no errors occur in the record of his
testimony."

Cukier stood. "On behalf of my fellow archivists, we welcome with
great respect the Chairman of the Jewish Council of Kalisz."

Hahn showed no pleasure at the greeting but spoke low, with a
marked accent and slow pace, far less eloquent than our own Eldest of
the Jews. "Before the war, the Jewish population of Kalisz was 23,000.
In the final quarter of last year, there were 700 Jews left."

We stared in disbelief at each other.

Hahn nodded his head sadly. "The mass evacuations began in
September of 1939. Children up to the age of 14 and those unfit
for work were taken separately." He paused. "We don't know where."

I never felt a chill like the one I felt now.

Hahn nodded his head again. "There are only 160 Jews left in my
town."

After a protracted silence, Cukier spoke. "I'm sorry for your people. It must be hard for you."

Hahn gazed at Cukier. "Our Council is still functioning, but of course, not on a scale as yours."

"Have you toured the Chairman's workshops?" I asked, not knowing what else to say.

Hahn gave me a weak smile. "Your gracious Chairman gave us a personal Order Service—that is what you call your police? We had a very nice guided tour. Your operations are well-organized. Impressive."

Heilig was taking mental notes.

Hahn sighed. "Rumors reached our ghetto that starvation among the immigrants here was rampant." He looked questioningly at us. "I'm gratified to hear from your officials that such rumors are false." He paused, studying our faces. "Your Chairman assured me that he applies a policy of "complete equality" toward all the ghetto residents." He looked Cukier in the eye. "How many of your people have been deported?"

How matter-of-factly he asked that. Always the numbers man, I rattled off, "Ten thousand. 4,853 men and 5,750 women."

Cukier added, "We have 151,000 Jews still here, thanks to our leader."

Hahn replied, "That is good to know. The Jewish ghetto of Kalisz is almost empty now."

"Can you stay here?" Rosenfeld asked. "I have four in my flat, I could make room for one."

Hahn smiled and shook his head. "You are too generous. I must return to my people. As long as there is one still there...I am responsible."

"May I ask you something?" I hesitated.

Hahn looked at me with a curious expression on his face.

"Is he right?"

I caught a warning look from Cukier but felt compelled to ask, "The Eldest of the Jews, Chairman Rumkowski, believes if we convince the

Germans that our ghetto is a manufacturing powerhouse, essential to their war effort, they will leave us alone. Is he right?"

Cukier was silent.

"I know it's just your opinion, but after all you've experienced, I really want to know."

Rosenfeld stared into Hahn's eyes.

Heilig leaned forward.

Hahn glanced at Cukier who nodded his head. "My friends, we thought we were safe too. As to your question, I don't know. Your Chairman is a strong leader, much stronger than we were. He spoke much of his efforts to protect his people, in the manner you describe. As I said, he is far stronger than…I was." He let out a deep sigh. "I would say, up to now, he has been successful. The future? Who knows?" He got up to leave. "I will tell you that I hope he is right. Only the Lord God knows."

I expected Rosenfeld to add, "The Germans know," but he was deep in thought.

"Have any of you ever been to Kalisz?" Hahn smiled sadly again. "It was a lovely town. It really was." He shrugged his shoulders and headed for the door. "God bless and keep you all."

After the door closed behind him, we were silent. What could one say in the face of such devastating news? A whole village of nearly 25,000 Jews had overnight become a ghost town.

Cukier broke the silence. "You see, it is as I have said repeatedly. Only the wise moves of our great Eldest of the Jews, Chairman Rumkowski, are saving us from a similar fate."

We went back to work, all joy drained from our bodies as if by Hahn, the vampire. I thought of nothing else for the remainder of the day.

That night, I crawled into bed and held onto Miriam as a child holds his mother fearing the monsters in the shadows of night. She did not pull away but pressed the back of her body deeper against me. Shortly before I fell asleep, I thought I heard her weeping into her pillow.

CHAPTER 7

F EBRUARY 21, 1942: THEY WERE DELUDED
A rumor spread through the ghetto that the resettlement was to be suspended. Unfortunately, the rumor proved false; resettlement proceeded according to the plan announced in advance...10,000 people were to be deported during the month of February. It is worth mentioning that among the deportees were a good number of socially harmful individuals...

The second resettlement order caught us off-guard. We thought the initial ten thousand would satisfy the German appetite for Jews. Most of the deportees had to be dragged forcefully. Wild gossip circulated. The deportees were no longer given German marks, so the rumor spread that they were going to places where they would not need currency. The truth was that nobody knew where the deportees were being sent. I'm not sure we cared. We were grateful not to be included. "The devil you know is better than the devil you don't."

I read the last paragraph of my entry again. "The resettlement in February was far more worrisome than the one in January. The guards ordered the deportees to throw away their knapsacks and the bundles they were carrying by hand, including food supplies they had taken with them for their journey into the unknown." I looked at Heilig. "I don't know if the Chairman will keep that last bit in," I said.

"I don't give a shit."

I was shocked. "What do you mean?"

He moved closer. "Don't you ever get tired of this?"

"You're new here. You're tired already?"

"I'm tired to death."

He reminded me at that moment of Singer. We still had no word of our young friend's whereabouts. Each notice of a suicide, escape, or shooting, I was afraid would include his name. Where the hell was he?

"February 3, 3:30 A.M., a resident was shot and killed at the intersection of Smugowa and Frandiszkanska."

Was it Singer? I waited anxiously for the name, for clues the victim's identity.

No. It was a 34-year-old woman shot when she had gotten too close to the barbed wire.

"February 18, 5:00 in the afternoon, a body of a man was found lying near the barbed wire. He'd been shot in the mouth."

Singer? Had he opened his mouth once too often? It could have been him. This victim was shot trying to enter the ghetto. Unidentified. So many were unidentified. Singer?

"February 24, 6:00 P.M. a bullet smashed through the head of a man near the barbed wire."

Singer? The uncertainty was unbearable. I sat on the edge of my chair and then sagged back. This poor soul was born in 1881.

Each day brought new tragic notices, electric shocks racing through me, fearing that it might be him. I couldn't imagine how this uncertainty was affecting Miriam. I wished I could console her, but that would be too difficult. Keeping busy was my only refuge.

Work in the factories was never allowed to be interrupted. Whispers circulated that a massive public meeting was to take place Saturday morning on the Square. The rumors proved correct. The German authorities issued an order to have the residents of all collectives and German Jews appear on the square at 10:00 A.M. Nobody knew the purpose of this assembly, but in the morning, I saw long lines of people, escorted by Order Service men, marching to the square.

Holding my government pass, I followed, intending to write about this unprecedented gathering. I stopped walking. Had the wooden gallows always been there? What the hell was going on?

The Order Service lined up the throngs of people in front of the skeletal structures. They ordered everyone to silence.

A cart drove through the crowd. I recognized officials from the Central Prison headed by Commandant Hercberg. I sensed what was happening but didn't believe it, didn't want to believe it.

Four Jewish policemen, yellow stars on their armbands and caps, escorted a heavily shackled prisoner from the cart. I saw only his back.

My guts twisted inside. The faceless man was the right size and build. Singer? Gallows?

The man was led up the wood steps. I was too far back to see his face. A few officials following him blocked my view.

I pushed forward but saw only the escort, the prisoner lost behind them. When they stepped aside, a German in uniform, armed guards flanking him, addressed the crowd. His voice thundered in the microphone.

I pushed closer to the front but still couldn't see the victim's face.

The German finished his speech. He moved to the side.

The hangman was now the only man near the gallows who was not wearing a yellow Star of David patch.

They're not going to do this, I thought.

The executioner slipped the noose around the condemned man's neck.

I grabbed the arm of someone next to me and hissed, "Who is he? Who is he? Does anyone know him?"

The answers came in nervous whispers. Some said the victim was a Pole brought in from the city of Lodz. Others rasped he was a Jew.

My questions were interrupted by someone shouting orders in German.

German police were standing on the stage and several meters away from the crowd. Their machine guns and rifles were aimed at us.

There was a strange, inhuman, moaning undercurrent, a few

sporadic curses, but much of the crowd was dead silent. Some dared to glance at the ring of riflemen. I was too frightened to look, to count the men who wanted to kill us.

There was a gasp near me.

I turned. The man was hanging, his legs kicking, his arms bound. I prayed he would die quickly, but his legs struggled to find the missing floor, kicking, kicking, kicking. And then they were straight and still. I was sick to my stomach. I heard a man barely audible, reciting Kaddish, the Mourner's Prayer. I had not said that prayer in years but recited it silently now…as much as I remembered. Most did not dare pray. It was against the law. Machine guns and rifles were aimed at us.

Two Germans on the stage took photographs of the hanging man, flashbulbs flaring.

A celebrity, I thought bitterly.

The German officers saluted, and straight-backed and razor-sharp marched to their automobiles. The cars left the square.

The crowd began to disperse, Jewish police watching for any ripple in the calm surface.

The body remained hanging.

I walked home on rubbery legs, tears threatening. I couldn't control them. I couldn't control anything. Was I insane? I couldn't go upstairs like this. I stared at our block of flats and felt such despair, such hate. I sat on the curb.

I don't know how long I sat like that. I was finally able to stand but was afraid my face would reveal all to Miriam. I walked back to the square.

The body was still hanging.

The poor soul is at peace, I thought, flinching upon hearing wheels approach.

Four adolescent workers pulled the wagon. Two boys climbed the steps to the high platform. One used a knife to cut down the body. The others caught it before it hit the earth. Together, they tossed the victim into the open maw of the wagon. Then all four pulled it away.

Soon more men arrived pulling a smaller wagon. They dismantled the gallows and hauled the wood away.

It was as if it had never happened. But it had.

If Miriam knew about the ghetto's first public execution, she never said.

Not having seen the face of the victim, not knowing his identity, unable to deal with what I never thought I'd witness, I could not tell Miriam. I was just grateful that nestled against her, I slept a few hours. I did not remember having nightmares.

The next day, as I walked to the Administration building, some residents by the notice board were whispering about the execution. "Did you hear his wife and daughter were forced to watch it?"

I thought of Miriam and little Regina being forced by Nazis to watch me swinging from the gallows. What monsters could do such barbaric things? Why would they do it? "Does anybody know who he was?"

A woman sidled close, her voice low. "His name was Maks Hertz, resettled from Cologne."

"A German?" I felt some relief at that news.

"Yes. He was a printer," someone else said.

"When did he get here?" I asked.

"He, his wife and nine-year-old daughter, arrived in October."

"That was the first transport. Do you know what he did?"

The woman scoured the area anxiously. "No. He was a neighbor. I didn't know him well, but I never expected this."

"I'm sorry," I said.

She grunted and hobbled away.

I saw an Order Service officer I recognized. I still feared these policemen but needed answers. I approached him with a congenial smile, my I.D. in hand. "Good morning, Jack," I said, trying to sound confident.

"Good morning," he replied.

"I'm writing a report for the Chairman. Do you know what this criminal, executed yesterday, did?"

The officer gave me a wary look. "You're government, so I will tell you what I know. Unofficially," he said, looking furtively around. "You will not use my name, or it will be bad for you."

"I swear. I just need the basics for my report. I can wait for the official police report but prefer live witnesses, experts such as yourself." A little flattery couldn't hurt.

He nodded. "The man was stupid. He slipped out of the ghetto and spent several days in the city." He stopped to survey the few zombies dragging their bodies around the periphery of the square, his club tapping against his gloved palm. "The fool was buying a train ticket to Cologne. He would have made it, except when he opened his wallet, his yellow patch fell out."

Shit! He was trapped by the Star of David.

The officer shrugged. "That is all I know." He turned to the zombies.

"Thank you. I appreciate your help."

He nodded and then said in a low voice, "I'm sorry for his wife and daughter. We live in terrible times." His face turned official again.

"Thank you. Be assured I will not mention your name."

Club raised again, he headed toward a small group of zombies. They scattered before he arrived.

I stared at the site where a man's body had hung from the gallows. It was now barren except for a few ragged denizens scrounging around for whatever crumbs might be found. I raised my eyes to God, thanking him that the hanging man had not been Singer.

I never told Miriam I witnessed the execution. She must have heard of it, but never once mentioned it to me. In a few days, I knew people would stop talking about it. Our first public execution, a terrible precedent, would be eclipsed by other news. I hoped it would be the blaring, glorious, headline that the war was over and Germany lay in ruin. I hoped someday soon I'd see Hitler hanging in a public square, a large yellow swastika carved into his naked flesh. I hoped...I hoped...

I had little hope left, but I still clung to it, much as Regina clung with her tiny fingers to my hand. Or was it me, desperately clinging onto her sweet fingers to find any hope in this terrible existence? I recalled Miriam's question after we had made love a year ago: "How can we bring a child into a world such as this?" It made me want to cling to Regina's hand and never let go.

CHAPTER 8

*M*ARCH 1942: SUICIDES
The universal mood of depression and panic that reigned in March as a result of the resettlement action provided fertile soil for acts of desperation.

"I like the way you wrote that," I said to Heilig, who was becoming a bit more open.

"Do you think that will be censored?"

"No. I think you captured the mood perfectly."

Rosenfeld sighed. "This has been a terrible month."

"You're right. We had 2,244 die this month, compared to 1,875 last month." I said.

"There were twenty suicides this month alone," Heilig added.

Cukier looked from behind his handkerchief, now perennially in his hand. "Did you say twenty?"

Heilig nodded. "Most involve jumping from buildings, overdosing on pills, poison, and hanging."

"Any young men in their late twenties or early thirties?" I dreaded his reply. There had been no word yet from Singer.

"Yes." Heilig gave me a curious look.

"You have a list of their names?" I took the sheet of paper and scanned it. "A husband and wife, a mother and son..." Singer wasn't listed. Had Miriam heard from him? Had he escaped from the ghetto? Was he rotting in some prison? It was odd how someone could vanish, and nobody would ever find out what happened to them. Jews were disappearing every day, and nobody could learn their fate.

"And now we come to the shootings," Heilig announced.

Every day he recited these notices. It was torture. Before Singer's disappearance, all the victims, tragic as they were, had merely been numbers. They were strangers. Now that Singer was missing, each roll call of the men and women shot by the sentries kept me clenched and listening.

"On March 8, at 10 P.M., a man was wounded by two rifle shots as he tried to enter the ghetto." Heilig read in his sing-song voice.

That could have been Singer if he was coming back for Miriam and Regina.

"His name was Marian Osiecki, a barber."

Not Oscar. Thank God.

"On March 12, a woman was shot at 5:30 outside the ghetto."

Where the hell was Singer? Had he been killed and pitched into a mass grave with other unnamed black marketeers? How does someone vanish like this?

Cukier crumpled a sheet of paper. "Damn them." He looked paralyzed, the document balled in his hand.

We were silent, helplessly waiting for our leader to tell us what had upset him.

Cukier put the paper on the table. He undid the creases, as he spoke, "I just learned many of the March deportees while waiting at the Radogoszcz station…they froze to death." He looked as if he was going to cry. "Frozen to death. Do you know how painful that is? Those goddamn Nazi bastards."

"Julian, how many?" I asked, seeing he was barely able to stand because of his recurring coughing bouts.

"What the hell does it matter how many? Do you want to count the damn corpses personally? They've been sent back to the ghetto. Damn them! Damn you and your endless numbers!" He burst into a fit of coughing and pushed my hand away when I tried to help him. "Leave me alone. Leave me alone." He grabbed his coat, and still coughing, holding the wall, pushed himself through the door.

I hurried after him.

Rosenfeld grabbed my arm. "It is not your fault, Engineer. He is ill."

I sagged against the wall. "Heilig, would you please check on Julian for me?"

Heilig grabbed his coat and left the room.

"He's a good man, this Heilig," Rosenfeld said. "I wasn't sure."

I wanted to say he's not Singer but kept that to myself.

Rosenfeld smiled. "You miss our friend, don't you?"

I was surprised. The professor had rarely mentioned Singer since his disappearance. "He was a pain-in-the-ass, but I was used to him," I replied, still conflicted by my feelings.

Rosenfeld smiled. "He was full of surprises…a good boy." He held up his gloved hands. "He got these for me, you know? I never asked how. It's funny how little I know about him."

I couldn't tell him that some of Singer's 'surprises' weren't that good. I also wished I knew more about his past. "Do you think he made it out of the ghetto?"

"If anyone could, our young friend would be the one. Did he tell you that was his intention?"

"Many times. I didn't think he was insane enough to try it."

"Is it insane to want to escape this place?"

"To risk getting shot?"

Rosenfeld never had a chance to reply. Neftalin was standing at the door, his hands shaking.

"What happened now?" I asked, bracing myself for more bad news.

"Twenty-five thousand more are ordered out from the ghetto," Neftalin replied in a ghostly voice. "They are demanding nine hundred per day."

Rosenfeld and I looked at each other in disbelief. "What the hell are they doing with all these people?" I asked.

"They claim they need laborers for their rural food production," Neftalin said.

"I wouldn't mind being a farmer," I commented, imagining Regina running through a field of vegetables, Miriam and I planting precious seeds in the dirt.

Neftalin said, "Engineer, be careful what you wish for. The devil you know is better than the devil you don't." With that, he walked out the door.

Neftalin had used my rationale for not wanting to chance the unknown fate of those selected for resettlement. My life, the lives of all of us, were in the hands of the Eldest of the Jews. He was, I fully accepted now, the only wall between us and the total annihilation of the ghetto. It happened in Kalisz. I had to put my faith in our Chairman. We had to believe he could protect us. Could he save the 25,000 now required by the Germans? That was a whole different question.

CHAPTER 9

A PRIL 1, 1942
the ghetto's population was 115,102. 5,204 people died in the ghetto since January 1.

"I told you they're crooks," Miriam hit me with as soon as I entered our dark flat. She was holding Regina, who was wriggling, eager to come to my arms.

"I just walked in the door," I grumbled.

She let out a laugh that in another person I would have judged as insane. "You haven't heard? Of course not! Your bosses don't want us to know."

"What the hell are you talking about?" I threw my coat on the chair.

"Hercberg."

"I'm sorry?"

"That shit, Hercberg, the chief of the Central Prison. He's been expelled from the ghetto. He and his whole look-down-their-noses family have been thrown out!" Another insane laugh.

"Impossible. Hercberg is the head of the Order Service and one of our leader's best friends."

Miriam screamed, "He was stealing everyone blind. They all are! From top to bottom they're all rotten." She was gloating, a vicious smile on her face.

"It's a misunderstanding." The image of Hercberg resplendent in his Commandant's uniform flashed before me. He was a tall man, as tall as Rumkowski, and his official cap made him look even taller and more authoritative. Everyone feared him.

"It's no misunderstanding. He and his family were escorted to the train this morning. They're gone! The cruel sonofabitch is gone."

"You shouldn't use language like that in front of Regina," I said.

Miriam stopped talking, studying me. She lowered her voice. "When my parents gave me to you, I was put off by your age."

"I know." I should not have been surprised that she fell for Singer.

"Benny, you are a good man, a kind man."

"Thank you." A bone at least.

"Yes, you are a good man. Perhaps a little unadventurous, but I saw someone who knew the world enough that I would be protected. That is the only word I can think of to describe the trust I had in you…"

"Had?"

Miriam aimed her dark eyes at me. "We should have left here when we could, but you refused to even consider it. Now, we have a child. We both depend on you. But you, the man I respected, are too naïve, too blind, to see the truth."

My temper was rising dangerously. My hand was a fist. "I'm not naïve. I'm not stupid. Blind? I see the truth, but differently than you."

"You trust our leaders. You place faith in false idols. Hercberg, the supreme being of the Jewish police force, was living like an emperor. He had three apartments filled with gold, food, and money."

"Rumors."

"Benny, he used his position to plunder the people he was supposed to protect. He added to the suffering we are all experiencing…all, except your precious Chairman and his cronies." She began to cry.

I wanted to embrace her, but she frightened me when she got like this. "Miriam, why are we arguing? Please stop? I will check tomorrow on these rumors. I'm exhausted. You're exhausted. Regina hears our disagreements. She senses our unhappiness. Please, for our child's sake, let's put them aside for one night? I promise I will check tomorrow and I'm certain that Hercberg will be at his office as always. Trust me. It is more rumors and lies. Let us have a night of peace?

For Regina's sake."

Miriam's voice was calmer. "The ghetto is emptying quickly. Every day, more and more people are deported. Does anyone know where they are sent? Do you? Why aren't you telling me?"

"Nobody knows. I don't. I promise. The Chairman said the deportees are being relocated to farmland in the north. Away from the war. That is all I know. That is all anybody knows."

"Farmland? That is what the rumors say too." She smiled. "What do you think it would be like to work on a farm? I don't think it would be so terrible."

I shivered, recalling what Neftalin had said. "Miriam, we must pray that we're allowed to remain here. You say I'm naïve, but I don't trust the Germans. I don't see them doing anything nice for their Jews."

"I'm tired of this flat and the endless lines for a bit of bread."

"Our population is half of what it was. Things are getting better. The war can't last much longer. Please, let's go to bed? Regina is asleep. You need to rest so you can care for her tomorrow."

In the dark of our bed, I found Miriam's stomach and held my arm around her. "I am your protector," I whispered. "I will never let anything hurt Regina and you."

The next morning, I verified from Cukier that Miriam had been correct. The chief of police, his wife, mother-in-law, and his three sons, had been driven to the train station by German police and taken away in a private cabin.

"Does anyone know where the Germans took him?" I asked, hating to have to tell Miriam she was right.

Cukier shook his head. "We don't know the fate of any of the people deported from the ghetto. We just don't know."

A few days later, the gossip spread that Hercberg had killed himself shortly after his departure. Unfortunately, no one could verify that. No one seemed sure of anything anymore. The guiding principle for me: "The devil you know is better than the devil you don't."

The resettlement continued. A thousand people were sent from the ghetto each day. They were without money, without baggage. Some, the dwindling number of volunteers, sold their worldly goods for bread. In my entry, I wrote, "Such tears, such wailing, such wrack, and ruin! The last possessions of ruined people going for a pittance."

Cukier didn't react to my lapse into emotionalism. He rarely censored anything now. We were not even sure if the Chairman read our entries. He was far too busy fighting the battles that threatened our lives.

I began to wonder if life outside the ghetto was better than the suffering here. People were saying that news had arrived from a few of the deportees. The word got out that those fortunate enough to be relocated had found better conditions. This calmed many of our fears and deportation did not seem so terrible an option. But how could we be sure?

"I want to read you what I wrote," Rosenfeld said. "I don't know if our leader will like it."

I stopped typing. It was rare to hear the professor's thoughtful voice these days. He'd grown feeble, often forgetful. I could almost see the bones sticking through his taut skin. His hair was thin and stringy, and his eyes were often dull, lifeless. He'd never regrown his beard after the Nazi soldier had brutally shaved it off. Singer had been incensed over that vicious attack.

Cukier stopped working. He frowned as if carrying the weight of the ghetto on his thin shoulders. He still defended the Eldest of the Jews, but with far less tenacity than before. The coughing had weakened him.

Rosenfeld cleared his throat. "While formerly the processions of emaciated old people and children with cadaverous faces made a macabre impression on passersby, now the eye has already grown accustomed to seeing carriages pass loaded with people who are more dead than alive."

Cukier was silent, so Rosenfeld continued, "Wrapped in rags, barely visible, they lie motionless on the wagons. Their blank gazes fixed on the sky, their faces bloodless and pale, hold a silent, but a terrible reproach to those who have remained behind and are bustling anxiously about the ghetto." His eyes teared up. "We are the walking dead," he muttered.

Cukier coughed. "Add this: "The ghetto is under the sway of uncertainty...everyone figures that he may be deported and is acting accordingly." He crushed his handkerchief in his hand.

"It is strange," I said, "The Chairman has not made one speech lately, not one authoritative word on the deportations."

Heilig said, "You're right. Until now, he's never missed an opportunity to speak in public."

Cukier closed his eyes.

Something was in the air, and for the time being, no one could tell what it was. There was no sign of Rumkowski. German soldiers were patrolling our streets. Corpses were lying unburied, naked in the snow. I stared into the future and prayed to God that at long last the war was ending. Uncertainty was a cloud covering the ghetto, but rumors provided thin threads of hope in our despair and fear. The smoke, black snakes, rising from the factories, was a sign that we were still alive and would survive.

CHAPTER 10

A PRIL 3, 1942: PASSOVER SERVICE
On April 3, during services for the Passover holiday, the Eldest of the Jews went to the synagogue at 23 Brzezinska Street, where he delivered a short speech for the occasion.

"That's all?" I asked Cukier. "What did he say? Did he talk about the resettlements?"

"I wasn't there," Cukier replied. "This is all that was on the memo."

Heilig asked the question on all our minds. "Do you think the Germans are serious this time? Have they really stopped the deportations?"

I thought back to March when the Germans had announced a suspension of the resettlement process and the ghetto had been seized with joy. Everyone had breathed a sigh of relief. Cukier had a rare smile on his face as he read the Chairman's brief announcement. Only Rosenfeld seemed unmoved. "It's true," I'd said. "The deportations are over." I could not wait to tell Miriam the worst was over.

Within hours, the authorities rescinded the ruling, and the Resettlement Commission was ordered back to its work. This new suspension was greeted therefore with skepticism. People were afraid to allow themselves to be carried away with false joy.

The door flew open.

Neftalin was standing with a sheet of paper in his hand. "The Chairman has ordered the police to inform the populace that the resettlement is over." He smiled broadly. "Dear friends, it is over. The

Chairman has announced it. It is official!"

As we made our way to the dining room, everyone was talking about the end of the deportations. We were like children, everyone expressing their relief, their joy. Even the sober Rosenfeld muttered, "God willing, everything's taking a turn for the better."

When we returned to our room, Neftalin was back. "The Resettlement Commission has been liquidated."

"Entirely?" I still didn't dare believe this miracle on the second day of Passover.

"There are a few tasks left, but yes, the Commission members are all being returned to their former departments."

"It's really over," Cukier said. "Thank God. Thank God."

"I saw lines of people carrying bags, walking back from the station," Neftalin said. "It is over. Thank God. Thank God."

Tears inexplicably began flowing from my eyes. I hadn't cried like that since I was a child. I tried to stop but couldn't. It was as if everything I'd been holding in was bursting through.

Rosenfeld placed his arm on my shoulder. I could barely feel it. It had no weight. "My poor friend," he said tenderly, "you have kept your emotions inside for far too long."

I replied, "44,056 people. Since January, that is the number of deportees that have left the ghetto."

"I did not realize so many," Rosenfeld said.

"Each day, every day, a thousand left. I was counting the days until we would be called too." I gave him a smile. "One hundred days and the entire ghetto would have been empty."

"Only one hundred days?" Rosenfeld looked surprised.

I nodded.

"What a weight you carry, my friend. Numbers. Always numbers with you. Don't you see how frightening it is to perceive all of life as mere calculations? I did not realize until you said it that our ghetto was only one hundred days from total liquidation. You've lived with that ever since this started. Haven't you?" He shook his head. "You are cursed, my dear friend. You see the future when I am locked on the present, which is bad enough, mind you."

I had never thought about that before, but he was right. I'd been counting down the days until the ghetto would be liquidated, calculating when the last Jew would be torn away from this barbed-wire enclosed slum. I had viewed indifferently the faces of those lined up at the train stations, those dragged against their will from their homes. Numbers, numbers only...

"Tell me, Ostrowski, in your equations, did you see when this old man would be taken? Do you know what number of days would have passed before we, the insignificant chroniclers, would have been drafted for this journey?" Rosenfeld shook his head. "Of course not. And now, the most important question, with all your ability to see into the future, did you also calculate, God, forbid, when your sweet Miriam, and your precious Regina—"

"Stop. Not them! Please, not them."

Rosenfeld shook his head sadly. "I've made my point."

For a second, many seconds, I hated the old man. But he was right. I'd lost the ability to see people. I only saw the numbers. It was safer that way. No attachments. No fear of losing someone I cared for. I thought of one person I particularly missed. He'd betrayed me but still...I loved him. I could hear his voice, his laughter.

Heilig interrupted my thoughts with his brittle twitter of a laugh.

"What's so funny?" I asked, eager for anything that would make me laugh.

"There's going to be a concert on Saturday. Everyone in society is expected to attend. Our Chairman will deliver a speech."

I heard Singer say, "What else is new?"

Walking home, I saw that the news of the end of the deportations had sunk into the small groups of people gathered to read the Chairman's bulls on the posting walls. Some were skeptical, but most were hugging, crying, congratulating each other on being among the survivors.

Why were they so happy? What was it they suspected happened to the deported? We had been informed that the deportees were all working on farms where food was better, conditions were better, so why did we cling to our slum of a ghetto?

Miriam greeted me at the door with a rare hug. "Is it true? Can we now breathe easier?"

I felt her tears on my cheek. "Yes, Miriam, it is true. The Resettlement Commission has been liquidated. Thanks to our Chairman, the ghetto has been spared. We have been spared. The worst is over."

After a while, Miriam pulled away. "There are rumors that the deportees were killed," she said.

"False," I replied, taken aback by this new fabrication to undermine our government.

Miriam smiled. "Nevertheless, my husband, you were right. The devil we know is better than the devil we do not." She took my hand.

The news made me hopeful. We were here. We could bury the past. I let Miriam lead me to our bed.

"Regina is asleep." She placed her hand on my cheek and kissed my lips. Her lips felt dry and cracked, but I held onto her as we dropped to the sheet.

Tears filled my eyes as we explored each other, held to each other, trying to keep our bed movements silent. She clutched me tightly as I pounded my body against her, seizing this rare moment when the stars, for once were perfectly aligned. Hungry, exhausted, fearful of the next day, I grabbed this opportunity as if it was our last. And for one short cluster of minutes, the war was forgotten, our differences were forgotten, Singer forgotten.

When Regina cried out, Miriam hurriedly arranged her shirt and rushed from the bed. Our interlude was over. The world had intruded on us in the cry of a hungry child.

CHAPTER 11

APRIL 15, 1942: A CONCERT
On Saturday, April 4, local society attended a concert at the House of Culture. Everyone was awaiting the Chairman's arrival and the speech he would deliver on the present state of affairs since the interruption of the resettlement campaign. Those expectations were, however, disappointed. This did not impede 'copies' of the speech that did not take place from being circulated the next day. According to one version, the leader of the ghetto was supposed to have said that a new resettlement was on its way.

Rumors were among our worst enemy. How they started, how they spread, frustrated our Chairman. He had repeatedly lashed out at the false prophecies, but often they portended truth, so every new lead spread uncertainty, fear, and depression.

Neftalin was a frequent visitor now. He was hungry for any bit of good news we had gleaned from our reporting departments. He brought us up to date when he could. Today, his announcement was momentous: "Nearly 70,000 Jews from Lublin have been resettled," he said.

My family was there. "Are you certain? The Chairman said this was another rumor," I remarked, having heard from Miriam this distressing information.

Rosenfeld said. "So, it is true?"

Neftalin's grim face was the best answer.

"I've heard some will be coming to Lodz," Rosenfeld said.

"That we do not know." The Deputy responded.

"Some say that the resettlement of Lublin means it will happen here too," I said. "If they can move seventy thousand… How many Jews are left there?"

Neftalin's voice quivered. "Less than five thousand, but don't draw any conclusions from that. We are an entirely different kettle of fish. The Germans don't want to disrupt our productivity—"

"Do you really believe this?" I surprised myself at how much I sounded like Singer. "To the Germans, a Jew is a Jew. They hate us."

Neftalin shook his head. "The Chairman has finally got some good news about our deportees."

I thought of Singer. "How did he get this?"

"He was visited by a commander of the camp where our deportees have been sent. This is the first definite source of information—"

"So, where are they?" I asked.

"The camp is near Warthbrucken. It used to be called Kolo."

"Kolo? So, the rumors were true?" I had to learn to trust the rumors more.

"The camp houses about 100,000 Jews including 44,000 from our ghetto."

"That is a large number," I said, still unable to understand why a country at war, like Germany, would spend time and resources on these mass resettlements.

"This camp was formerly occupied by German soldiers. Perhaps 30,000 lived there. They say the barracks are in decent condition and furniture remains." Neftalin handed Cukier a sheet of paper.

"What about food and work?" Rosenfeld asked.

"The officer claims the food is plentiful and those fit to work are employed repairing roads and doing agricultural tasks." Neftalin smiled. "They're talking about setting up workshops modeled after those the Chairman has wisely established here."

"Is that where the Lublin deportees are also being sent?" Rosenfeld asked, glancing at me. "There are persistent rumors that all seventy thousand will be sent here."

Cukier looked at Rosenfeld. "Things are just starting to improve here. We still have typhus and hunger. Surely the Germans are aware of these problems and will not dump such a large number of immigrants on us?"

"Nothing is definite at this time." Neftalin rose from his chair.

Cukier coughing made him barely able to speak, but he managed to ask, "The Chairman canceled his speech.. yesterday at the concert. Today, it was announced... he was going to speak again... at Krawiecka Street, but he canceled again."

"What is your question, Julian?" Neftalin asked, concern on his face. "Take your time, my friend." He looked at me.

I shook my head but didn't want Julian to see.

Cukier coughed into his handkerchief. "You know my question," he managed to croak before another coughing spell.

Neftalin surveyed our faces. "You've all been loyal supporters. I've read your reports, and for the most part, they are not only accurate but show understanding of our precarious situation." He lowered his voice. "I will share with you the truth, but it is only for you. He canceled his speeches because we do not know what to make of the news from Lublin. Even the Eldest of the Jews does not know. We never contemplated such a massive movement."

"So, they could be settled here?" Heilig said.

Rosenfeld supplied his usual answer, "Only the Germans know."

Neftalin smiled sadly and left us to suffer another bout of anxiety.

As the rumors spread of the Lublin liquidation, and the possible influx of seventy thousand new hungry immigrants to our ghetto, depression again took its grip on us. All eyes and ears were waiting for some definitive word from our leader. There was an unusually long silence, a fog cloaking the ghetto in gnawing uncertainty.

CHAPTER 12

THURSDAY, APRIL 18, 1942: AN INSPECTION
At around 2:00 P.M., high-ranking representatives of the authorities visited the ghetto, their inspection announced a few days in advance. In the course of two hours, the inspectors visited the following enterprises of the Eldest of the Jews: the textile workshop, a hide and leather workshop, a carpenter shop, and a boot-top workshop. Eyewitnesses state that the inspectors left with a most favorable impression after visiting the local enterprises.

Cukier thanked Neftalin for the note and handed it to me.

"You see, the Germans are again impressed by our productivity, more noteworthy under these difficult circumstances," Neftalin said and left the room.

"There is hope," Rosenfeld said. "The Germans were impressed." He looked ready to spit on the floor.

Cukier croaked, "Deaths?"

Heilig, the ghoul, had the reports. "Sixty-six deaths yesterday. 37 men and 29 women. Do you want to know the causes?"

Cukier waved his hand.

I saw dried blood on his fingers.

Heilig bent over the page. "5 died of dysentery, 2 of lung disease, 2 of nervous ailments…8 of old age, 1 from loss of blood, 16 heart attacks, 11 exhaustion, 7 of heart problems related to exhaustion, 1 of cancer…2 of other causes."

"That's only 55," I said.

Cukier lowered his handkerchief. "The numbers man never rests. You left out tuberculosis."

Heilig glared at me. "I must have missed it. My eyes are not so good lately." He searched the page. "Here it is. 11 of tuberculosis."

"11?" Cukier repeated. "In just one day?" He smiled benignly at Heilig. "Please, do not leave it out again?"

I felt like an idiot. How could I not have realized why Heilig had deliberately omitted the deaths caused by tuberculosis?

At lunch, I followed the Weasel to the latrine. Checking to see the stalls were empty, I did what I should have done months earlier. "You are doing a good job," I said, giving him what I hoped he would take as a friendly smile.

"Thank you."

"I...I didn't realize why your numbers did not add up this morning. I was foolish."

He glanced at me through his thick lenses. "You couldn't know."

"I should have. I love Julian and should have realized why you were doing that. I'm sorry."

Heilig nodded.

"I'm also sorry I did not do more to welcome you."

"I understood. The good Doctor told me about your feelings for my predecessor. I would also resent someone who was taking over for a friend who is missing."

"He wasn't my friend. Well, maybe he was." I no longer knew. "Singer was outspoken, a bit of a rascal. I envied him. I guess I was jealous of him."

Heilig looked uncomfortable. "I must go. Lunch is over soon." He left me just like that.

I wondered if I had done things to him he might not forgive. Had I done that to Miriam too? And yes, to Singer?

After lunch, I noticed a bit of commotion at the bulletin board on the Square. I crossed over and saw a new proclamation, No. 374, announcing that all above the age of 10 not working would be given medical examinations.

"It's a trick," a female zombie whispered. "They want to eliminate the sick."

Her comment was enough to stir up angry retorts and violent threats against the governing body, especially the Chairman, "who attends concerts while we must take phony medical examinations."

I hid my identification and brushed my way through the crowd. I hurried to our chamber. "Have you heard about the mandatory medical exams? It's causing a great deal of anger."

Rosenfeld looked frightened. "You don't know?"

"What don't I know?"

He leaned closer. "The doctors doing the examinations are all Germans."

That afternoon, there was a loud uproar outside our building. Thousands of people crowded the square.

I jumped when the door swung open.

Neftalin rushed into our room. "It's pandemonium out there. Go home. Go early today."

"What's going on?" I asked, grabbing my coat. "We haven't finished."

"Thousands of people are rioting for work papers. It's too late. The Chairman has been begging everyone able to register for work all along. Did they listen? He begged over and over that only work would save us. The medical examinations threw them into a panic. They stormed the Bureau of Labor, but it is shut down, not taking applications. It is too late…too late."

"Surely, something can be done to help them?" I said.

Neftalin shook his head. "The Eldest of the Jews saw this day coming. Go home, my friends. Thank your Chairman that you are under his protection for your labors on behalf of our residents."

As I left the building, I saw a column of police, clubs at the ready, advancing toward Lutomierska Street. I headed in the opposite direction. Everywhere I looked, people were moving toward the Balut market, the square that housed the Ghetto Administration offices. I had never seen the ghetto so filled with anxiety and anger.

When I ran up the stairs and opened our door, Miriam and Regina weren't there. Panic raced through me. Where were they? My wife had been increasingly despondent, believing every rumor that her friends shared with her young ears. I ran down the stairs and back into the street. Where would she take Regina?

The sound of a rifle shot reached my ears. The barbed wire! I ran. But realizing I could be the next victim of a bullet, I forced myself to slow down, walk quickly. No running. No running. I reached the end of Zgierska.

A shape was hanging on the wire. A body.

Hands reaching to the top rail of the fence, a woman hung, trapped by the barbs. Blood flowed from where the sharp teeth were buried in her flesh and from an ugly hole in her back.

Ice in my heart, I stepped closer. Where was the sentry? I was still far enough away.

Her head fell back, eyes upside down.

Thank God! Thank God! It wasn't her. It wasn't Miriam.

"Get out of here, filthy Jews!" The German sentry shouted, pointing the barrel of his rifle at us.

I should have screamed at him, "Butcher! Monster! God will punish you!" I should have tried to free her from the barbs. I backed away. No longer quite human, I backed away.

I climbed our staircase to the flat I hated. Falling on the chair, I stared at Regina's crib. I saw that poor woman, her dress shredded and reddened with blood where the barbs ensnared her, torn wide open with the crater where the bullet struck her spine. I pounded my fist over and over on my knee. "God, why are you doing this to us?"

When Miriam came in with Regina, I felt faint with relief. "Where have you been? I went searching for you." I couldn't lift myself from the chair. "Thank God you and Regina are safe."

"He's coming back," Miriam said.

"Who is?"

The excited look on her face supplied the answer.

CHAPTER 13

APRIL 29, 1942: SEWING MACHINES
Have arrived in the ghetto in great quantities over the last few days. On the basis of evidence in the form of notes and printed matter found in the drawers of these machines, one may conclude that they were sent here from small towns in Kolo and Kutno counties.

It had been a week since Miriam reported that someone saw Singer in their travels to Warsaw. She was like a schoolgirl with the news. "He got out of here. I told you it was possible."

Singer was trouble for me when he was here, and when he wasn't. In her excitement, Miriam must have forgotten that she never informed me of her relationship with our adventurous friend. *Friend?* How could I still believe that? "It may have been a false siting. You know the rumors—"

"Most are true." Miriam had that angry, stubborn face, but it quickly dissolved. "He's found a way to get us out. He's coming back for us. I know he is." She picked up Regina and swung her in a circle. "Regina, you will soon know freedom."

What could I say to her? Mathematically, I knew the odds were against Singer escaping. The odds were even more stacked against him that he would be able to return. I couldn't tell her that. I also couldn't puncture her momentary elation, by revealing I knew of her affair. All this animation dredged up the memory, the hurt, the anger, but seeing the long-missing bloom of life in her eyes, I couldn't burst her balloon. I'd continue to bear the pain on my own. For Regina's sake, I wouldn't reveal what I knew. Would Singer? Would he tell her about his letter, hidden in my briefcase?

I couldn't wait to escape. Even the tedium of our work was better than the tension of keeping secrets from Miriam.

Cukier was reading a report about the on-going medical examinations when I arrived. Weakened by his stubborn coughs, I suspected he was reporting to work every day to avoid what we all feared, our bodied being examined by the German doctors. "They give everyone a bowl of soup free," he said. "What else do we know about these inspections?"

Rosenfeld leafed through several eyewitness reports. "A few German doctors and Gestapo representatives were present."

"Yes, but administrative functions were performed by officials of the Eldest of the Jews and the Jewish police who kept order," I said, reporting something I'd read in the reports from the police department. "The women were examined on the top floor of the soup kitchen at 32 Mynarska Street and the men in the hall below."

Cukier asked. "Were they told to remove their clothing?"

We all searched the reports.

Heilig replied, "Anyone over sixty was not."

"Thank God for that," Rosenfeld said.

We all laughed at his shriveled face.

Rosenfeld stopped laughing. "It says here the doctors stamped a letter on the chest of everyone examined."

"What kind of letter?" Cukier asked.

"There were 16 letters, 8 for men and 8 for women. An L for women meant they were unfit for any work."Rosenfeld looked upset. "This is unheard of! Doing such things to our women?"

"I saw the Germans take a few hundred elderly patients from the Old People's Home," Heilig said. "They were barely able to stand in the long lines."

Cukier frowned. "Children under the age of fourteen are also being examined. The Chairman has begun a campaign to have children over the age of thirteen work as apprentices in community enterprises." He looked up from his notes. "He is trying to protect the children. He always protects the children."

Neftalin burst into the room. "Good, you are all here." He looked at Rosenfeld. "Remain here tonight. Cukier, you too."

"What's going on?" I asked.

Neftalin looked extremely uncomfortable. "The Germans are not happy with the number of people showing up for examination. They complained to the Chairman and issued an ultimatum that if more do not show up for the mandatory exams, they will bring them in themselves. The Chairman, backed against the wall, has no recourse—"

"What did he do?" I asked, an alarm ringing wildly in my brain.

Neftalin murmured, "He had no choice."

"What did he do?" I leaned forward.

"The police have been ordered to find anyone hiding from the exams."

Rosenfeld shook his head. "Our police are forcibly bringing people for exams by the Nazi doctors?"

"He had no damn choice!"

"How many?" I asked.

Neftalin pulled a sheet of paper from his coat pocket. "I knew you would want to know." He glanced at Cukier. "You should be fine. You are employed and underage." He glanced at Rosenfeld. "Doctor, you should remain here…until this is over."

Rosenfeld smiled. "The Engineer asked you how many?"

Neftalin unfolded the paper. "About 1,500 were brought in by the police. 9,000 were examined…65% women." He seemed unable to decide what to do with the paper. "You must understand, the Germans demanded 20,000."

Rosenfeld stood slowly.

I had noticed recently how much older he looked. He was barely able to stand without using the table for support or leaning on a cane.

"I'm going home," Rosenfeld said softly and walked to the door.

"Please, stay here?" Cukier said.

It was too late. Rosenfeld was gone.

Neftalin handed me the paper. "I'm truly sorry," he said and left the room.

Cukier coughed into his handkerchief. "I'm going home too."

"You should stay," I said.

Cukier smiled and holding his head high went through the door.

Heilig and I were alone. He looked uncomfortable. He always did when it was just the two of us.

I gave him what I hoped was a reassuring smile. "I guess it is just the two of us to finish. I admire your amazing memory."

Heilig fidgeted in his chair. "I must tell you something." He really looked like a weasel, his eyes darting to the door. "A friend told me this in confidence."

"Go on."

"My friend is employed not far from our building. On Wednesday, he observed a large truck had stopped to refuel." He glanced at the door again, and then into my face. "The truck was fully loaded with luggage."

"Luggage? What do you mean?"

Heilig leaned closer. "There were many kinds of bags, but mostly knapsacks." He looked meaningfully at me. "The kind belonging to the people recently resettled."

"So what?" Why he was bothering me with a truck full of luggage.

"They looked used."

I didn't understand. "They could have been new," I said.

"My friend said the bags were full."

I fell back in my chair. "Are you sure?"

Heilig nodded.

"Where did you say the truck came from?"

"From the area of the camp at Chelmno," Heilig said. "My friend saw the manifest."

"Many of our residents were sent there." I felt a chill. This couldn't be right. I had to fight what I was thinking. "Heilig, this is third-hand information. We can't spread such rumors without proper authentication."

"But what do you think it means?"

"I don't know."

Heilig moved back to his corner and ducked into his work.

I went back to my work, still mulling over his report.

Suddenly he mumbled, "The Gestapo tortured me."

I looked up, so shocked I couldn't think of anything to reply. Heilig had been a stranger to me, and now this admission made me see him as even more alien. Why did he say this now?

Heilig's eyes met mine. "The Germans are capable of anything," he said.

I waited for more. Nothing came. "The Germans are capable of anything." I didn't want to think of what he was hinting at. Could a truck full of filled knapsacks have some other explanation?

There was an uncomfortable silence between us the rest of the day.

When I walked home, the streets were deserted. It hit me that many flats were now empty; neighborhoods vacant. I remembered the hollowed-out faces, the zombies, the old people that had filled this area. In a flash of lightning, I saw a truck, its container over-flowing with used knapsacks.

CHAPTER 14

MAY 1, 1942: LUGGAGE

On Wednesday, a few people employed at Balut Market observed a large truck that had stopped to refuel en route from Zgierz to the city. The truck was fully loaded with luggage of various sorts, but chiefly with knapsacks belonging to the people recently resettled from the ghetto. The truck was allegedly on its way from Kutno to Pabianice. It is difficult to determine whether or not this information is accurate. Thus, the bulletin notes it with obvious qualification.

"You wrote that well," Cukier said.

"I guess after so long working with you, I'm learning," I replied.

"That last sentence should get this past our censor," Heilig said. "It clearly raises the necessary question."

"Will he answer it?" I asked, believing still in the Chairman's special relationship with the authorities.

"I don't know if he knows," Cukier replied. "Have you seen the latest proclamations? Doctor, do you have Proclamation 380? It is on yellow paper. We've run out of white."

Heiling interjected, "We've run out of everything except his proclamations."

Cukier shot him an irritated look.

Rosenfeld pulled out the yellow sheet. "I've already written about this. It pushes the latest immigrants to the front of the resettlement lists. The native Lodzer have been all employed by the Chairman, while the immigrants remain vulnerable as they are unemployed."

"He has tried to create jobs for them," Cukier said, exhausted at having to defend the Chairman's actions.

Rosenfeld sighed. "I would not want to be working at picking up excrement after having held prominent positions. That, and five months of hunger, cold, and sleeping on bare floors, has resulted in a number of these immigrants volunteering for transport from this *paradise* of ours."

"The problem is nobody knows where these people are being resettled," I muttered. "And still our population is dropping. As of today, we are down to 110,860 people. 48,068 men, and 62,738 women."

Singer would love the odds, I thought, wondering if that would have kept him away from my wife.

"I wish I knew where the others were sent," Rosenfeld said.

The way he said that alarmed me. "We are safe," I replied.

Rosenfeld eyed his pipe. "The medical examinations are still going on."

Heiling shook his head. "They finished today."

"Too late," Rosenfeld said. "The Order Service police have been dragging long-time residents from their homes for the examinations."

I was about to respond that he didn't have to worry when Neftalin burst through the door. "Damn them! Damn them to hell! Twenty thousand more they want!" He slammed himself into a chair. "Twenty thousand more."

We were stunned. The silence was sending all sorts of thoughts into my brain.

"It won't be us," Heilig said.

"I don't know who it will be. Everyone is saying it's someone else. The Commission has made up so many lists that no one has a sense of anything—whether they are sending those well-enough to work or the sickly. The foreign Jews are in despair, and no matter how our Chairman tries to reassure them, nothing stems the terrible rumors. I tell you, my friends, it is a mess. We must all pray that the Chairman can protect us."

I was struck by Neftalin's sudden uncertainty. "I can't imagine they would take the recent arrivals. The majority are walking shadows. They'll never be able to make the journey."

Rosenfeld, our own 'walking shadow,' spoke softly, "Do you think the Germans care about such concerns?"

Cukier's voice was shrill, "Our Chairman is hoarse from warning everyone. He is like Moses when the ancient Jews worshipped false idols while he received the Commandments. They don't listen. They seal their own doom." He burst into a fit of coughing.

I hesitated to ask, but Neftalin seemed more open than usual. "Henryk, have you heard of a large truck carrying luggage from the camp at Kolo?" Did his facial expression change? Was he glaring at me? I had to persist. "Some say they saw thousands of knapsacks, the kind many of our people took with them when they left us."

"I have to leave," Neftalin said abruptly. He rose to his feet.

"Have you heard of this truck?" I repeated. "Has the Chairman?"

Heilig jumped before the door.

Neftalin stared at him for an instant and then turned an icy gaze on me. "We have heard the rumors, but that is all they are. I have work to do. Excuse me, gentlemen?"

I joined Heilig at the door. "Please answer? You call us your friends."

Cukier looked surprised. "Henryk, you know about this?"

Neftalin turned back to me. "You, of all people, Engineer, know we must rely on fact, not speculation."

"A truck full of used luggage is a fact." I was annoyed at his evasiveness.

"Did you see the truck?" Neftalin asked, glancing at the door still blocked by us.

I shook my head.

"Do you know anyone personally who saw the truck in question?"

I remembered Henryk was a lawyer before all this started. From his cross-examination, he must have been a good one. "No. I don't know anyone personally."

Cukier sighed. "It is another baseless rumor. I'm sorry, Henryk."

"I know someone who saw the truck," Heilig said.

Neftalin smirked. "And you trust this so-called witness?"

Heilig nodded. "You know him too."

Neftalin hissed. "I know no such person."

"You do, and so does everyone in this room." Heilig pulled out a folded sheet of paper.

"I have no idea who you mean," Neftalin said, making to pull Heilig away from the door.

"Who is this witness?" I asked, staring at the square of paper Heilig handed me. I almost fell over when I saw Singer's name.

CHAPTER 15

MONDAY, MAY 4, 1942

On Monday, at around 8:00 A.M., the first transport of the Western European Jews, who are being resettled after being settled in the ghetto a half year ago, pulled out of Radogoszcz sidetrack station. At the moment, one important detail has been established in connection with the departure of the first transport: all those departing consisting of one thousand people had their baggage, knapsacks, and even their hand-held parcels taken away from them. This news has cast a chill over the ghetto.

TUESDAY, MAY 5, 1942

The second transport of Western European Jews left today. Their baggage was taken away from them, as it was from those who left yesterday.

WEDNESDAY, MAY 6, 1942

Today's transport, the third of the new Western European Jews, one thousand people, was also completely dispossessed of its baggage.

It had been three days since I was shocked to see Singer's handwritten note. Heilig was a stone, refusing to reveal how he got it from our former friend.

"I want to know where Singer is," I demanded, cornering the Weasel against the wall.

"In good time," Heilig said, looking frightened, but refusing to yield.

"I've been worried sick about him. Is he in the ghetto?"

"He's been in and out," he replied.

"I don't believe it! I want to see him, now. Tell him that."

"I'll try. But I can't promise anything."

"You tell him his god-daughter wants to see him." I pushed away from the wall. What kind of rat doesn't make any effort to see his god-daughter...or Miriam, I thought. I never hated anyone so much. In my mind, it was two plus two equals four.

After we confronted Neftalin with Singer's report about the trucks, he took the note and said he would bring it to the Chairman. We had not seen him since.

Two days passed, and each day, I found a moment, nobody around, to corner the Weasel. "Did you see him? Did you tell him? Did you tell him his god-daughter misses him?" I didn't reveal anything yet to Miriam. How could I hurt her with false hope?

The Weasel twitched, but he revealed nothing more.

"You'll tell me," I said and held a fist near my belt.

Thankfully, the door opened, and Rosenfeld entered. If he suspected anything, he didn't show it.

All day, I felt as if I wanted to beat Heilig until he told me what he knew. Fortunately, for him, Rosenfeld and Cukier never gave me a chance and Heilig left early, allegedly to cover some story related to the resettlements.

I was lost in thought as I walked home, past boarded-up shops. I felt something hard slam into my back. A German rifle. "I have a new baby," I thought of crying out. Anything to save me.

"The alley," a voice growled, the gun barrel pushing deeper. "Not a sound, Engineer."

"You!" I twisted around, my fists ready to smash against his face, but he wrapped his arm around my neck and squeezed hard. "Get in there." He dragged me into a thin space between two buildings. "Shut up. You're not in danger." He dropped the pressure on my neck. "I'm letting you loose, but keep quiet."

"You bastard." I rubbed my neck, still not believing it was him.

"We must be careful," Singer said. "Don't say anything."

"You, sonofabitch," escaped my lips. "How could you do that to me?"

"Later for that. I have important information—"

"I don't want your damn information! Where have you been?"

"I said later. This is urgent. I have no time. Please listen?"

"Regina misses you. Miriam…" I choked on the words.

"Listen for heaven's sake!" He gripped my collar. He was stronger than I remembered. His eyes were rimmed by dark circles, and his face was brown, weather-beaten. He smelled of sweat, not like him. His clothing was black, and he had a black beard. Was it the playboy? He pulled me toward him. "There is something strange going on with the deportations."

"I don't care," I said.

"Shut up and listen. The Nazis are lining up the deportees at the station. They order them to throw all their baggage to the ground."

I was attentive now. "All of it?"

Singer nodded. "Their knapsacks and suitcases but also hand-held parcels. Everything."

"You saw this yourself?" Unbelievable. He'd been here all along?

"Yes."

"Maybe they loaded all it onto special train cars—"

Singer peered down the alleyway. "No. The Order Service, under watch by the Gestapo, gathered it all up onto wagons."

"They were our police?"

"Yes. But they were being watched by armed Germans."

"It doesn't mean anything." I was desperate. "Maybe there was no room on the train. Did the wagons follow the direction of the train?"

Singer shook his head. "I followed the wagons to the Office for Resettled Persons on Rybna Street."

"That's strange. Back into our ghetto?"

"Yes. Everything was unloaded into storehouses there." Singer looked me in the eyes. "The same buildings where I saw the trucks with the used knapsacks."

"You've been spying here? How long? Why haven't you contacted us?"

"Not now. You must get this to the Chairman as soon as possible. I'll be back." He made to move out of the alley.

"You didn't answer my questions." I gripped his coat, but he easily pried free of my fingers. "Answer me. For Miriam's sake!"

He held my hand in a cruel twist. "Don't make me hurt you? We don't matter right now. Please? I promise we'll talk, but I have much to do, and so do you, my friend."

I was about to scream that he was no friend of mine, but he was gone. He was like a shadow, moving stealthily into the unlit streets of the ghetto.

Concealing this new information from Miriam would be too difficult, so I avoided all but necessary conversation with her. It was easy to fake depression. It was everywhere.

That night, when Miriam went to bed, I remained in my chair. I thought of the deportations and Singer's troubling information. Many residents had expressed their belief that whatever fate waited in the resettlement camps was better than the struggle for some semblance of life in the ghetto. How would they react if told them I had verified proof about the truck full of used luggage? I wished I could inform them about the deportees being forced at gunpoint to relinquish their modest possessions. I wanted to tell Miriam, but it would kill her to know Singer was near but did not come for her. How could I deliver such a blow to her hopes?

The next morning, I stopped at Neftalin's office. He didn't look pleased to see me. Another friend who wasn't a true friend, I thought as he invited me into his office.

"What can I do for you, Engineer?" He asked, remaining on his feet.

I handed him the folded paper. "Is this from Singer again?" He began to read. "You put me in an awkward position the other day," he said.

"That was not my intention." I had to choose my words carefully.

He was the second most powerful person in the ghetto. I couldn't afford to alienate him. "We have been loyal to you and our Chairman and deserve the truth."

Neftalin folded the paper. "Did he say anything else?"

Neftalin listened to my report about the truck in stony silence. "Oscar Singer gave you this information?" He asked, his eyes weary.

"He said the Chairman must be told."

Neftalin smiled, but it was not a warm smile. "The Chairman has warned us many times that such rumors are enough to interrupt our productivity. You know any such disruptions would invite more calamitous actions by the authorities. We must avoid any panic at all costs."

"But this confirms our fears. The rumors are true. Our Chairman must do something."

Neftalin placed his arm on my shoulder. "Leave this information with me. You can be sure I will report all this to the Chairman." He prodded me toward the door. "Thank you for your loyalty."

I was out the door before I could protest. I thought of going back and demanding to see the Chairman myself, but Neftalin had been the one who hired me. I doubted if I could get an appointment with the Chairman without going through his Deputy. I had to trust him. Was I overly suspicious? Was that what Singer and Miriam had done to me?

I never discussed with the others my meeting with the Deputy and never was told what Neftalin, and the Chairman did with my report. The Deputy was right about one thing; the wave of rumors already spreading about the deportations, combined with the evidence of the trucks, was enough to cause a cloud of uncertainty and intense fear that shadowed every day of our existence.

I was grateful Singer was alive but wondered how long it would be before he contacted Miriam. Would he be able to save her and Regina? I no longer mattered. It was only Miriam and Regina who deserved a full and happy life. If Singer could get them out, that would be enough for me.

CHAPTER 16

MAY 6, 1942

During the last resettlement, the local Jews were forbidden to take their packages with them and people's knapsacks were cut off their backs...schooled by the experience of recent days, some people have struck on the old idea of putting on a few suits, a few changes of underwear, and quite frequently two overcoats. They tie the first coat with a belt from which they hang an extra pair of shoes and other small items. And so their faces, cadaverously white or way yellow, swollen and despairing, sway disjointedly on top of disproportionately wide bodies that bend and droop under their own weight. They are possessed by a single thought: to save the little that remains of what they own, even at the expense of the last of their strength. Some people have become overcome by utter helplessness, whereas some still believe in something.

"It is powerful," Cukier said, choking back coughs and tears.

Singer had written it but asked me not to reveal that I had seen him. I hated taking credit for his work but understood its significance.

"I did not know you could write with such emotion, and yet, it is understated." Cukier rocked back and forth slowly. "Do you still believe the war will end soon, Engineer?"

"I don't know. How can a maniac such as Hitler stand up against the entire world?" It was inconceivable that such an evil man could endanger the survival of so many innocent people and still not be stopped by the combined forces being raised against him. "I don't know," I said again. "Do you?"

"I do not know anything anymore. I had such faith in our Eldest of the Jews, our Chairman. I had such faith…" He let out a deep sigh. "Type it as is. You have voiced our emotional state well. I thought you were only interested in numbers. I underestimated you as the world underestimated the madman of Berlin."

Rosenfeld nodded. "Who is to say who is mad these days? If the whole of Europe is enflamed with insanity, then we, who are not, are the ones who may be judged insane."

I shook my head. "I would never believe we could come to something like this. It makes no sense. It defies logic."

Heilig frowned. "There will always be a need to hate someone. Hitler has tapped into that hate and has made Germans believe all that is wrong in the world is the fault of the Jews. There is nothing new in this. I suspect one hundred years from now Jews will still be hated. It is our fate."

Rosenfeld shook his fist. "What is new is how far one madman has taken this. Who knows what will come next?"

"The Germans know," I said, mimicking the professor and began to type.

"I think we should include this in its entirety," Heilig suggested, after reading a report by a Jozef K. "Just listen to how he describes the Germans from Hamburg who arrived here six months ago and left on the last transport." He straightened the paper. "It is only an excerpt. He first describes these 'newcomers' as snooty, dressed in elegant clothes, resentful of their poor conditions here, but then says, 'And indeed, it was only half a year, only six months, that had proven to be an eternity for them.'"

Rosenfeld interrupted. "It's true. Each day is an eternity. It is hard to believe all this horror has taken place in such a compressed period. Please go on?"

Heilig found where he left off. "Some of the metamorphoses could not be imagined, even in a dream…Ghosts, skeletons with swollen faces and extremities, ragged and impoverished, they now left for a further journey on which they were not even allowed to take a knapsack."

Cukier interrupted. "This has all been verified now?"

I nodded. "We have witnesses, including several Order Service men who were forced to collect the belongings strewn all over the ground by the train station. Some of them were in tears." Did I care about the emotions of others? What was happening to me?

"Another instance where the rumors have become fact," Cukier said bitterly. "How much more can I take?" He gazed at the blood stains on his handkerchief. "God, how much more?"

The periods of silence that now occurred regularly during our discourses were painful. They gave too much time to think, to reflect, to contemplate the all too near future and to give in to hopelessness, and despair. In this painful gap, I thought of Miriam and Regina. I could see them playing in the small park, my little girl running. My sweet child, almost a year old already, kicking high, propelling her swing into the air, always under the loving eyes of my Miriam. Was she my Miriam?

"Engineer, where are you?" Cukier's voice punctured my daydream. I snapped back to the present. "I'm sorry."

"No need. It is good to escape once in a while, my friend," Cukier said. "Please, Heilig, continue? We are all here now." He gave me an understanding look.

Heilig continued, "'They had been stripped of all their European finery, and only the Eternal Jew was left...'" He paused. "This man can write. We should hire him."

"Only the Eternal Jew was left," Rosenfeld repeated thoughtfully. "It's true. No matter how we fool ourselves into thinking we have escaped, our essential being, by fancy dress and by our attempts at assimilation, at the end, when all else is stripped away from us, what is left? Our Jewishness...only the "Eternal Jew." It is the one indisputable truth of our existence that even the Nazis cannot destroy."

Cukier smiled sadly. "In two words, this Jozef K has summarized all our history, our efforts to assimilate, to improve the communities in which we forever live on the treacherous periphery. Though subject to pogroms and outbursts of hate, often when we feel most immune to such things, we survive because we stubbornly return to our essence, our faith. The fact is that no matter how we believe we are protected, we will always be regarded as Jews, reviled as Jews for reasons I shall never understand."

"Our faith is our blessing and our curse," Rosenfeld said. "But I believe it is also our salvation. Without our faith in God, how would we survive? What are we without it? Dust."

"Dust is right, but under their boots," Heilig said.

I was silent, once again, awed by these far more articulate and educated scholars. All my life, I thought I'd succeeded in leaving my Jewishness behind. How could I, a rational, logical, engineer, a believer in science, make immutable, foundational, mathematical truths compatible with a heritage I had come to denigrate as ancient superstition? Everything in my life and career had steered me away from my legacy, my origins, convincing me that I was a Pole, a European, a non-denominational being, who was Jewish only by birth. My religion was an accident that meant little to me other than for identification, mostly by others. But the truth was, that as much as I had denied it, I was painted by my "Eternal Jewishness," not just in the eyes of those that hate Jews, but in something deeply embedded in my very being. "He's right," I said. "Once all else is taken from us, and there is nothing left, we still have our faith."

"Even you recognize this?" Cukier said. "Then the world is doomed."

"That's funny," Heilig remarked without smiling.

"What's funny?" Cukier asked, echoing all our wishes to find something humorous in all these catastrophic piles of papers that nobody would ever see.

"Listen what his last sentence is: "The premonitions they had that first Friday in the ghetto had proven all too true."

The last sentence hung with me as I made my way home. The

collectives that had housed the immigrants were now ghostly, all deserted. Stripped bare of humanity, no sign of life, the doors yawned open, waiting for their next transient lodgers. It was as if the very wood of the floors, the fading walls, the dust-laden windows, all knew everyone and everything was temporary. These rooms that housed thousands were immune to feelings for those they lost. Were we becoming like the inanimate objects decaying around us, no longer sensitive to the anguish of others?

Regina was playing on the floor when I got home. I sat on a chair and watched her smashing her doll made of rags against the wood floor. Over and over, her tiny hand smashed the poor faceless figure against the hard earth. It was as if she hated it. I turned to Miriam to see if she was watching.

Miriam's eyes were aimed at the door. She looked tired but poised as if she expected someone to soon enter. When she caught me studying her, she averted her eyes from the door and toward our daughter. "Don't do that to your baby," she said in a voice weakened by hunger and hopelessness.

Regina looked up, gave her mom a half smile, and then proceeded to bash in the rag skull again and again.

CHAPTER 17

FRIDAY, MAY 8, 1942: *A MUCH SOUGHT-AFTER ITEM*
Potato peels have become a much sought-after item...the only nourishment apart from bread for some people.

"How can people live on such meals?" Miriam asked. "Even the soup kitchens are struggling. Porridge is cooked on odd-numbered days, while canned beet or sauerkraut soup is prepared on even numbered days. Hunger is everywhere, except—"

I was too exhausted to fight with her. Rumkowski had warned me the first day that people would hate me if they ever found out what I knew and had not shared. I suspected Miriam, though she didn't voice it, harbored some degree of hate for me and all those who kept the ghetto running. She made no bones of hating the Chairman. She had taken Singer's place in spiking every mention of his name with a barb about privilege and inequality. She could not accept that we had to provide a little extra for the officials or the whole house of cards would collapse. It already was teetering. I was losing patience with my obstinate wife and all the armchair critics. They didn't understand the desperate circumstances facing our leader.

"Soon the whole damn ghetto will be emptied of all the poor immigrants," Miriam continued, her attacks unrelenting. "But your master will still be in his fine coach, smoking like a chimney, eating caviar and Vichy champagne, and listening to Wagner at live concerts—"

"Enough! Enough!" My shout caused Regina to jump.

Miriam scooped her into her lap. "You're upsetting her."

"I'm not. You are. You are incessantly nagging at me about things which you know nothing about! You and your yentas have no idea what is going on—"

"Stop shouting," she barked, holding Regina against her, eyes squinting up as if about to cry. "You're always on his side."

"Just stop already!" I rasped. I had to calm myself, for Regina. "If it weren't for the Eldest of the Jews, I would be unemployed, and we would not be here. I have no idea where they would send us. Why don't you understand that? It's simple. Two plus two equals four. Are you too stupid to see that?"

Miriam looked shocked, her lips quivered.

Regina, a frightened look on her face, her arms wrapped around Miriam's waist, was all that was stemming Miriam from exploding in anger. I saw it in her eyes and her expression. "You're one of them," she said as if pushing a knife into my heart.

"You're right, I am. And that is all that is saving us."

Miriam glared at me, "I should have left with him when he asked me."

I fell back into my chair. It was out in the open at last. How to handle it? What could I say? I examined her face to see if I could detect any sign of remorse. Instead, I saw a twisted version of my young wife, her face a mask hardened by resentment, forged by despair. "I have to go to work," I said softly and rose from my chair. I felt old, sick, as I bent down for my battered briefcase, barely able to restrain myself from striking her. If my child had not been in her lap, God knows what I might have done.

Miriam barely looked up, clutching Regina to her soiled shirt, to her broken heart.

I did not even kiss her forehead. Had Singer been present, I would have stabbed him, stabbed him, stabbed him, until he was dead.

As I walked, I saw a column of what looked like several hundred Jews heading toward the rail station. I ducked away from them, afraid of being grabbed up by the Jewish policemen and being forced into the line.

German police were at various points, observing, ready to act if a Jewish officer did not respond to any infraction by the silent marchers with enough force. Clubs and kicks were prodding the stragglers.

I did not want to watch. After Singer's report confirming the continuous stream of rumors, we all suspected the worst for these wretched people. It was odd how Singer's reappearance, even only that one instant, torpedoed every one of my hopes: my hope that I could reignite my marriage; that the thousands who left our ghetto were now safely ensconced in a better place; and finally, that we could outlast this awful war. On the one hand, Singer's spying—that is what I called his secretive actions—had provided vital evidence that all was not as the Germans made it appear, but it had also wreaked havoc on my attempt to pretend my life was bearable. Our playboy had done away with all of that. But I could not hate him. The truth was I wanted him to reappear if only to assure me he was safe.

At work, I think we all had the sense that we were on a downward slope, our feet on ice, the Germans waiting for some signal to propel us toward whatever lay at the bottom of the abyss. Rosenfeld was more sullen, obsessed by reports of the resettlements. He was the one who now counted all those beings called to the train station. Our kind professor was the one who listened attentively to every witness to the discarding of luggage, especially the treasured knapsacks. His writing showed his emotional bond with the victims as he spoke about the long wait at the train station and the atmosphere that he described as "profoundly tragic."

I kept my eyes on Rosenfeld's face as Heilig read an entry about the most recent transport: "The impression is of people waiting for either a reprieve or a death sentence. Tears of joy or of terrible despair—everyone reacts one way or the other upon hearing his name called."

"It's like Judgment Day," Rosenfeld said, examining a hole in one of his gloves.

"But God separates the good from the evil," I remarked. "The Germans make no such distinctions."

"God is merciful," Rosenfeld said. "It will be good to be with God...soon."

A few months earlier, I would have clobbered him with protests over his fatalism, but none came to my brain. I too sometimes wished for an end to all this. I could only imagine how much worse it was for my old friend, aged by being deprived of his wife Rosa's companionship, aged by expecting his name to be called.

Cukier said, "God isn't merciful if he allows all this. Don't talk to me anymore about a merciful God! He's a selfish shit who is taking pleasure at punishing us for nothing we have done. You, Engineer, you were right after all. There is no God." He fell forward on his handkerchief, racked by coughing. "How much longer?"

I put my hand on Cukier's quivering shoulder. "No Julian, I was wrong. I see it now. The Nazis deny God. That is why they can do what they are doing. Without God they convince themselves they are gods. They determine what is right, what is wrong, who shall live, and who shall die. My dear friend, I was completely wrong. God will punish them."

The door opened.

I leaped from my seat, expecting more German inspectors, a constant now in our work environment. They charged in, glanced at our table piled with papers and one cantankerous typewriter, muttered some unintelligible shit in German, and stormed out. Unfortunately, their contemptuous sneers remained in my memory for hours after. We never knew if a visit would end with them rousting us from our cramped sanctuary and hustling us to the train station. Would Miriam miss me? Would she mourn her little ghost of a husband? For Regina's sake, I stood at attention and prayed.

Neftalin entered the room. His face was grim. "There are new rumors that another resettlement is about to take place."

"Not again." I just had admitted my belief in God, and the sky falls on us again?

"They are just rumors at this time," Neftalin said.

"How many do they want?" Cukier asked.

Neftalin sucked in his lips.

I could barely hear him when he said, "90,000."

I gasped, unable to fathom how this was possible.

Neftalin added. "I should have said, we've already sent 45,000. They want 45,000 more."

"45,000 more?" Cukier asked. "Where will we get them?"

"Damned if I know. The Chairman negotiated. He begged and pleaded, arguing that our factories, their military's lifeblood, would not be able to function..." He sighed. "They lowered their demand to 25,000 more."

"Where will they get 25,000 more of us?" I asked, fearing his response.

"We're working on it. We have no choice. The first group will be from those previously examined by the German doctors." He smiled. "We are all safe."

I turned to Rosenfeld, but his face gave no clue as to what he was thinking. His hands, veins blue lines barely concealed under a thin layer of skin, were spread flat on the table, his precious gloves stuffed in his coat pockets. It was strange how suddenly I wished I could see his old pipe hanging from his mouth. Without that pipe and his beard, the once distinguished looking professor looked like a tired and frail old man.

Neftalin shook his head. "At least, we here are all safe...for now."

CHAPTER 18

T UESDAY, MAY 12, 1942:
WHERE ARE THE JEWS?
This is the question sent here by the Jewish Council of the town of Inowroclaw. From its card, it is evident that the council has its seat in a monastery in the small town of Mogilna. They inquired as to whether the Jews who were 'resettled' in October of last year might be in our ghetto.

"Nobody knows where they are," Neftalin said. "All we know is that the ninth transport left our ghetto today."

"If each transport holds one thousand people, that means 9,000 Jews have left in this latest series," I said.

Neftalin nodded. "New resettlement cards were sent out today. It is a limited number, mostly undesirables."

Rosenfeld muttered, "We're all *undesirables* to the Germans."

Neftalin looked flustered. "I should not have used that word. You are right, Professor. Thank you for correcting me."

Was this mere lip-service? From the start, the Chairman made it evident he viewed anyone undermining the smooth operation of the ghetto, even with were once legal actions, as an "undesirable element," the first to be discarded if the authorities called for more deportations. Had the Chairman and his Deputy modified their views?

Rosenfeld rubbed his hands together.

"Does anyone know where they are resettling all these Jews?" Heilig asked. "The number is enormous, so where can they put them?"

Neftalin shrugged. "The few reports we get are inconclusive. The

92

Chairman is frustrated, but still fights for every Jew to remain here."

"But it is his police that are enforcing the German demands," Heilig said.

Heilig looked tired, more like a weasel than ever. He mentioned having been tortured, but I'd never pursued that with him. I could not be his friend, not after being betrayed by the love I bore for Singer.

Neftalin straightened. "Be careful of your words, young man. If what you say is true, you know it is because there is no option. All our actions have been to save as many as we possibly can. That has always been our mission. That is what your records reflect...must reflect."

"Why? Nobody reads them." Heilig voiced my frustration.

Neftalin stared at him. "I understand you have doubts of the importance of your task. Frankly, I never imagined that the war would last this long."

"I never did either, and you know how good I am with estimates," I said.

Neftalin sighed. "It fooled us all. But someday soon, with God's help, it will end, and when it does, people will want to know what happened to the Jews of Europe, of the Lodz ghetto. The future will need your work to understand how we worked to overcome whatever the Germans heaped upon us." He shrugged his shoulders and brushed a hand through his thinning hair. "And, I suppose, there will be questions...many questions...some of which may be difficult to answer." He paused, surveying our faces. "If your words survive, if your testimony is read, at least some of those questions will be answered." He began to walk to the door and then stopped. "I know each of you is judging our actions. Some of you have concerns. I don't blame you. I do as well. But history will be the ultimate judge, and your work may be the only evidence. That is why the Chairman has entrusted this mission to you. It is why you risk your lives chronicling these events under the noses of the authorities. When the time comes, we will find a way, I promise you, to conceal your documents, so your children and grandchildren, and future generations will honor our valiant struggle to keep this bastion of Jewry alive in the devastation of Hitler's war against Jews." He laughed. "I sound like a Rabbi giving a sermon."

"It is needed," Cukier said. "We need a pep talk."

I nodded.

Rosenfeld remained silent.

Heilig said, "I didn't understand before. I honestly thought these old jokers were kept in such luxurious quarters simply to keep their precious brains safe from the Nazis. And they are remarkable brains." He gave us the first smile of affection I ever saw from him. "Thank you for including me. You are right. I have doubts about some of the decisions made, but now I am committed to this mission. I want the future to appreciate what we suffered so it will never be allowed to happen again to anyone."

Neftalin lifted an imaginary glass. "To the future."

"To the future," we repeated, hoisting our own invisible goblets.

Cukier announced, "We have work to do. Go Henryk, back to your world of high pressure. We great minds need to focus on the task at hand."

As Neftalin left, I heard him mutter, "You have no idea."

Heilig held up a sheet of paper. "Are you ready for the suicides? We have a 'Frenzy of Suicides' today."

It was amazing how that man could bring me down.

"It looks like we have ten." Heilig continued.

"A mob gathered in front of the soup kitchen fighting for potato peels," Rosenfeld interrupted. "The Chairman decreed that no more potato peels may be issued to the people of the ghetto."

At the visual of so many zombies scrambling over each other for potato peels, I burst out laughing and couldn't stop. I also couldn't stop the tears that followed the laughter.

"He's insane," Cukier said.

"We all are," Rosenfeld replied, staring at the hole in his glove as if that would mend it.

The only time I genuinely felt joy these days was when I held Regina on my lap and told her a story. I made them up, avoiding any tale that might frighten her. When she looked up at me, clutching her rag doll, all seemed as it should be. She sucked her thumb, perhaps from hunger. I thought she understood, in some visceral way, the distance between her parents, now seemingly unbridgeable.

Some afternoons, Miriam would leave the flat for several hours if I came home early. I never asked where she went. Occasionally, she'd return with a few bits of bread, a candy or two for Regina, ersatz coffee for me. I wondered where these things came from but didn't ask. It wasn't that I didn't care. I cared too much. So, I didn't ask. While she was gone, Regina and I would play a game of hide-and-seek. I would hide her in the closet, and she would wait silently until I found her. "You must be quiet. Shaa. Do not move." She would burst like a balloon into happy giggles when I made a big deal of finding her. I'd swing her to my chest, where I held her against my heart until we played our funny game again. And again. I knew it wasn't funny, but Regina loved it.

At night, I often sat in my chair, listening to the sound of Regina breathing. It was the music they took away from us when they confiscated our radios. It was the music that rose like a tiny prayer to God. I couldn't understand how any God could hear that sweet prayer and not be moved by it. Surely soon, he would give in and answer my daughter's, and every child's prayers. How could he resist?

CHAPTER 19

M AY 18. 1942
Between the 4 and 15th of May, twelve transports containing 10,915 people left the ghetto. 94 people scheduled for resettlement died. Twenty-five people were sent from the hospital and 300 volunteered.

The chair was vacant. It had been for two days.

"Is the doctor ill?" I asked.

Cukier didn't reply.

Heilig looked up from his writing. "They took World War I veterans. I saw them, old men, barely able to walk, hobbling with great pride. Many wore their iron crosses and medals for wounds and actions as they marched military style, four abreast." He stared at me and said, "Nobody is immune. Not even war heroes."

I leaned toward Heilig. "Have you heard from our friend?"

"He's like a ghost, showing up when he chooses. He gave me this note for you."

It was sealed. It wasn't what I hoped for. I folded it and slid it into my pocket. It was a report of another transport. "I want to see Oscar. Can you get a message to him?"

Heilig looked nervous. "Did you see they are giving free potato peels to anyone with a medical form?"

I turned and saw Cukier staring at us. Had he overheard us? "Potato peels? It shows how hungry we all are. No one ate those before. Now there are huge lines at the soup kitchens…for potato peels. Miriam makes soup and flat cakes from them. Our ration cards we use for Regina." I could almost hear my little girl crying from hunger. How could the Germans hurt children with angel faces was beyond me.

"I will see if we can increase your rations," Cukier said and promptly coughed hard into his cloth.

I no longer looked when he coughed like that. It must have been so painful. I'd grown fond of him and could not bear that someday his chair might be empty. I turned to where Rosenfeld sat. I could almost see his gaunt face bursting into a good-natured smile. I could see his hands rubbing together, always cold, even in his tattered gloves. "Has anyone seen the Professor?" I asked.

Cukier frowned. "You already asked that."

"I did? Yes, I remember."

"Are you alright, Engineer?" Cukier asked.

My sick friend was asking me if I was okay? "Yes, as well as can be expected." How well could I be without sleep and with crumbs for meals? How well could any of us be waiting on tenterhooks for our names to be called to be removed from this Eden of ours and shipped to God knows where? The picture of trails of luggage left by the railroad tracks haunted every minute of my existence. "I see Speyer died," I said, trying to refocus on our task.

Heilig frowned. "The scientist?"

"I knew him," Cukier said. "He was a great man. I would guess he was in his early sixties."

"63," I said.

"Cause of death?" Cukier sighed. "He discovered Eukodal, a major improvement over morphine in pain management."

"Exhaustion and weakening of the heart, the report states." I shook my head. "At age 63? He worked for many years with the German drug company, Merck. You would think they would save someone so valuable to them?"

"Imagine how many great minds the Germans are losing in this senseless war," Heilig said. "It's a damn waste."

"It is a waste," I agreed. "I don't understand it. Just today 57 people died. One more was killed by a sentry. The poor man lived in a building near the barbed wire, and they shot him for that."

"I wonder who invented that fence shit," Heilig asked. "I'd like to hang him by his balls on those barbs." He burst into bitter laughter. "I bet it was a Jew. We invent everything."

"Was DaVinci Jewish?"

"Of course not," Heilig replied, looking puzzled. "Maybe he was. That would explain a lot."

"He wasn't Jewish," I said, laughing.

"Then we didn't invent everything," Cukier said.

"Einstein is Jewish," Heilig said.

Cukier replied, "He was smart enough to get the hell out of Germany. I should have listened to my uncle from Chicago, but who would believe such a thing possible?"

I didn't say anything. I knew I should have left long ago. If I could find Singer, it might not be too late. Even if I could get Miriam and Regina out...that would be enough.

Neftalin was standing outside our door when we left for lunch. "I was about to come to you," he said. "We have news. A transport of approximately 4,000 Jews has arrived here from Pabianice. Most are men and women in the prime of life." He looked uneasy. "The thing is... the children have been separated. They were sent off in another direction."

"Did they know this was going to happen?" I asked, alarmed at this news.

"As the newcomers tell it, they knew nothing of this deportation. The majority were professionals, highly regarded by their employers."

"So why would they be sent here?" I asked, trying to make sense of the German's decisions. There had to be some rational reason for all this.

"Nobody knows. They were doing work for the military, but from what some said, the orders slowed down. They blamed corruption of their Council of Elders for much of the trouble." Their Chairman was arrested, and his Council deported for skimming off monies supposed to be paid to the workers. That does not happen here. Our Chairman acts quickly if such corruption is discovered. Even his closest colleagues, such as Hercberg, found he was not above the law."

"You said they were working for the Germans?" Heilig asked.

"Yes, until the ghetto was closed down," Neftalin replied. He must have seen the alarmed looks on our faces because he quickly added, "That can't happen here. Our ghetto is far more valuable to the Germans. The Chairman has made us a model of manufacturing productivity. The Germans can't do without us."

"Excuse me, Henryk," I said, a burr sticking in my brain from his earlier statement, "Am I correct that you said the children were not sent with the parents?"

Neftalin looked at me. "I will tell you what I was told, but remember, it is from just a few of the new arrivals. It is in no way authoritative." He paused. "I understand your concern, my friend, but you mustn't worry. That will not happen here."

"Please tell me what you know?" I saw Regina's face.

"On the 16th, a Saturday, the workers and their families were ordered to assemble in front of the buildings where they lived. I believe it was in the early evening. They were then taken in groups to the Krusche and Ender Company's athletic field. They were told a census was being taken. They were not ordered to bring anything with them, and in fact, didn't even dress for the Sabbath, but wore their working clothes."

"They thought it was just a census?" Heilig asked.

Neftalin nodded. "They were ordered to line up into groups according to the letters they had received during recent medical examinations."

"Shit! Like the ones we had here," Heiling said.

"Most likely. The people with the letter "A" and those with valid working papers were ordered to one side, while the unfit, aged, sick, the children, those marked with the letter "B" were placed on the other side."

"Children were separated from their parents?" My stomach clenched.

Neftalin looked kindly at me. "This is why we must be grateful to our Chairman. Engineer, I don't know...this hasn't been verified. I only met with a few of the deportees, so we can't be certain."

"Children were separated from their parents," I repeated, unable to contemplate something so horrible. "Tell me the truth? No more hiding the facts. What really happened?"

Neftalin looked at the door, sighed, and said, "We're not sure of anything, but since you want the truth." He let out a deep sigh. "My friend, from what we know, and we know very little, children were not allowed to go to persons in group A." He hesitated. "They said infants were torn from their mothers... children ran crying and screaming around the field looking for their parents... parents begged the guards to allow them to take their children with them..."

"My God," Heilig said and aimed his eyes at me.

I saw Miriam refusing to release Regina from her arms. "What did the guards do? Surely they took pity on these children?"

Cukier said, "Engineer, don't worry. It won't happen here."

I was trembling. "Please, what happened? The guards must have done something to help?"

Neftalin rubbed the bridge of his nose. "I'm sorry. No. They shoved the mothers back. The children were torn from their arms and thrown to the grass like balls...some were even thrown over the fence..." His lips quivered. "None of this has been authenticated. We must hold onto hope..."

I leaned on the wall, afraid to hear more, but knowing I had to. "What happened next?"

"The adults were kept on the field. It rained. They were all drenched. They had nothing to drink or eat. They were numb with the loss of their children. Many hours later, they were told they were going to our ghetto."

"And the children?"

"Nobody knows."

"Nobody knows?" Cukier asked, "How can nobody know?"

"From one newcomer's report, we know the Germans selected one hundred men to help the weak, the elderly, and...children onto wagons." Neftalin's lips quivered again. "Those men never returned."

"And the children?" Why must I keep asking?

Neftalin shook his head and aimed a sad expression at me. "I will tell you because you ask. It is terrible to see these desperate, lamenting women and men wringing their hands from which those nearest and dearest to them were rudely torn. Most do not eat, and did not reply to our questions—"

"So, it is possible the children will still appear?" I asked, clutching to hope.

"That is what we are telling the newcomers. The Chairman himself is investigating this." He smiled at me. "You need not worry. The Eldest of the Jews, our brave Chairman, would never allow this to happen here."

"Thank you, Henryk." I squeezed his hand.

"You must trust the Chairman," Neftalin said. "He loves our children."

I watched him leave, remembering the first time I saw him. There were only a few occasions when he still had that swagger and authoritative appearance of that first meeting. The successful lawyer he had been now looked as if he too had been beaten down by all the bad news we had suffered. Where were the angry young men of barely a year ago? I turned to Heilig, to beg him to find Singer for me, to plead with him that it was urgent our last hope contact me.

The Weasel had vanished.

CHAPTER 20

M AY 21, 1942: *FALSE RUMORS*
   A rumor which has the whole ghetto talking concerns a resumption of resettlement that is to begin on Friday...the rumor specifies that children and people stamped by the medical commission will be the first to go. The Chairman categorically denies this report.

I was late. Miriam and I had gotten into another of our arguments. It had begun the night before when she confronted me with the horrific rumor that some Jews had been taken into our ghetto, but without their children. I tried to deny the truth, to spare her from the fear I now felt for our Regina. When she preferred to believe the rumors more than her husband, I exploded, shouting that she and her friends knew nothing of what was going on.

"All I want to know," she screeched at me, "Is it the truth? Just tell me the truth?"

"I already told you it is not verified."

"Stop lying! I can't trust you! You're a liar! This is our daughter we are talking about!"

Regina turned toward the sound of our arguing.

Her eyes melted me. "Okay. I surrender." I lowered my voice. "I was trying to spare you."

"Don't protect me by lying. I want to know so we can do something—"

"I've tried. Believe me, Miriam, I've tried." I couldn't bring myself to tell her I had begged Heilig to get Singer to meet with me, over and over. I'd begged and begged.

"You know what you must do," she said.

I felt myself about to explode again. "Why don't you contact him? You're the one he loves. He wants you and Regina." I felt Regina's eyes on me again and lowered my voice. "It's okay. I understand. If you can find him…do it…I'll be fine. I'll survive." I tried to smile, but how could I?

Miriam became quiet. "How can you believe your friend would do such a thing to you?" She looked deep into my eyes. "Do you believe I could hurt you like this?"

"It doesn't matter. If you can find Singer, I want you and Regina to leave."

Miriam shook her head sadly. "You're a fool. I thought you were only protecting me when you refused to leave the ghetto when I first asked you…then when Singer asked you. Now, I know why. You're a damn fool." She never raised her voice. She walked away and sat next to Regina on the floor.

I wanted to shout that I'm not a fool, that I know the truth. I couldn't. I felt as if I was a fool, for trusting them. No matter how much Miriam protested, I knew she loved him. I didn't blame her. I left the flat but did not head directly to work. I had something else I had to do.

On my way, I bumped into a Jewish policeman, with whom I had struck up a more-or-less friendly acquaintance. I gave him a furtive wave.

The tall officer looked around and then nodded his head.

I approached but stayed a short distance away. "How goes it, Max?" I asked, looking straight ahead.

"I'm sick of this shit," he whispered, lips barely moving. "Did you hear about the last group dropped in here like garbage? No children." He glanced at me. "I have five children…five."

"It's a rumor, not verified. I asked my superiors," I said.

"Consider it verified." He glanced at me. "Administrator, I feel for these sad people. Thank God for our Chairman."

I nodded.

He looked at this club. "I must go. Orders." He started off and then paused, his back still toward me. "Pray for our Chairman," he said. "Pray for all of us."

I was afraid to approach him again. God knew what orders he was rushing off to execute.

I reached my destination. I hesitated, checking around me. Nobody near, I hurried up the three stairs and gaped at the front door. It looked as if it had been bashed in by hammers...or rifle butts. I listened for the sound of boots. Nothing.

Terrified, I leaned into the small foyer. The doors on the first floor were all open. I smelled rotting food. Peeking inside, I saw a chair lying on its side, a couch with deep gashes in its seating, pillows torn and scattered around the room. There was broken glass sparkling against the bare floor boards, rugs tossed into the corner. All were threadbare indications that life had existed within these walls until something unexpected had ripped every being from the apartment.

"Oh God, no." I raced upstairs, suspecting what I'd find.

My friend's door was ajar. The wood surface was cracked, badly dented.

I pushed the door gently with my shoe. It inched forward. I didn't want to look inside.

The apartment appeared as did the others as if it was waiting for life to return.

I pushed the door open all the way and cautiously entered. A few photographs on a small reddish wood table were still standing. I picked one up of the good Doctor and his Rosa. They looked astonishingly young. Rosenfeld looked proud, his wife's hand on his arm, his well-groomed beard and tailored suit giving him a professorial appearance. I put it back on the table.

There was a bookshelf. No books. All confiscated. A once stately desk leaned for support against the wall under a boarded-up window. The desk drawers, poorly aligned, were dangling in space, no longer able to close fully, their contents were strewn on the floor. A few papers, all blank, rested on the desk surface as if waiting for the writer to return. An ink stain had spread and dried across the desk's surface. It reminded me of a puddle of blood.

I held the top sheet of paper up.

A pencil on the floor.

Rubbing the pencil's point lightly over the top sheet, letters formed. I folded the paper and placed it in my pocket. I took one more object. On the floor, under the desk, I found the bowl of Rosenfeld's ever-present pipe. I picked it up, tears welling in my eyes. Unable to leave this precious relic, I placed it in my pocket.

In the closet, I searched for his heavy coat.

The coat and gloves were gone. Thank God. He must be wearing them. My wise friend was always cold. He used to say, "Old men feel the cold more than you youngsters."

My shoes crunched on shattered glass fragments near the bed. The linens were strewn haphazardly, much dangling on the floor. The mattress, murderous gashes in its surface, had been pulled partly off the frame. I leaned over and stared at the sheet. Were the stains blood? He'd been in bed. Did he resist them? The puddle of blood was a clue, but not definitive.

The dresser drawers had been thrown to the floor, their contents in all corners. There was nothing worth taking. The wolves had gotten it all, and now they had our dear Professor.

I stood in the middle of the offensive silence. Tears formed in my eyes. It sank in slowly that I might never hear my wise friend's calming voice again. I recalled how I'd misjudged him that first day we met. I thought he was pompous, self-centered, an old stuffed shirt. He knew his time was near. Like everything else he had done, including sending his dear wife, Rosalie, to England before Hitler invaded, he faced the inevitable with quiet courage and dignity. At least that's how I preferred to see it. I'd never find out for sure.

I closed the door, closing off this part of my life. From now on, I would include him with my parents, Miriam's parents, when I said Kaddish, the Mourners' Prayer. Tears still in my eyes, I left the barren building, my hand clutching the pipe bowl in my pocket. I swore that someday I'd find out what happened to my friend, but now it was almost curfew and I was late.

The streets seemed darker as I walked in the shadows of the tenements. It was soundless, thousands of residents cowering in fear that at any second their number would come up. How can people sleep knowing their door may be smashed in by ruthless wolves without hearts and souls?

"Get into the alley," a raspy voice commanded.

"Is it you?" I stared ahead, a gun barrel in my back.

He shoved me hard, so I almost fell against the wall. "In that door."

It was dark. He was behind me. "Singer? Is it you?"

He shoved me against the wall. A match lit. His face looked demonic, wild. A black gun was in his hand. The sight of it made me stiffen with fear. "I followed you. Are you crazy? It's past curfew."

"Did they take him?" I asked. "Rosenfeld."

Singer lowered his gun. "I don't know. The Order Service thugs pulled 500 people from their apartments. Did you know that? It was under orders of your damn Chairman."

"No. He would never do that."

Singer's voice was menacing. "Of course he did. Are you still so blind?"

I was furious. I'd been blind, damn blind. "If Rumkowski did order that, it was because he was under orders from the Germans. He has to obey, or things will get much worse," I countered.

"Same old engineer." He brushed back his hair which was long and looked damp. "We'll discuss politics when this is over." He brandished the gun in front of me. "Why do you want to see me?" He kept looking at the mouth of the alleyway through the boarded window.

"I want you to get them out."

"You want that now?"

"Yes." I knew I was handing Miriam into her lover's arms, my Regina with her. "People have been arriving from other ghettos...without their children. I would never believe anyone could be so heartless."

Singer let out a bitter laugh. "They're not human. Haven't you seen that by now?"

I felt like throwing myself into his arms, begging for mercy. "Please, Oscar, please save my Regina and Miriam? I know you love them." I could hardly speak. "I do too."

Singer rubbed the barrel of his gun in his hair. He sounded more subdued when he said, "I can only try, my friend. The Germans are closing the noose on this sorry place. I'm stuck here myself. Do you remember the trucks full of sewing machines?"

"I vaguely recall that."

"I was hidden in a false compartment in the bottom of the truck, under the machines. We haven't been able to do that again."

"You must try. For the sake of Miriam and your godchild." I was aware that what I was asking might be impossible. It wasn't fair that I was asking him to risk his life.

Singer's breath smelled strong, almost fecal. He did not look the same, cheeks dark and hollow, jaws tight, thick stubble, eyes fierce, darting to the window, then to the door. "There is a price on my head."

"What do you mean?" His wild eyes frightened me.

"You wanted to know where I was. I was working with the resistance."

"You? The socialist? The pacifist?"

"I kept telling you we need to fight these monsters. Well, I found a band that is fighting them. I will ask if they can help." He pulled away from me. "I will find a way. How is Miriam? Are she and Regina strong enough to travel? It will not be easy."

There was love in his voice. I should have felt resentful, jealous, but I had failed them. I didn't deserve them. "Since you vanished, Miriam has been a shadow of herself. Her depression is deep and contagious. Regina is adorable, growing more like her mother every day. Thankfully, she has my intelligence, but Miriam's looks. She is like a small mirror of—" I looked up. He was gone. "Singer? Singer?"

Would he help us? Had I sent him away by my loving descriptions? Had I reawakened any bit of conscience he might still have? Had I by doing so cost my wife and child their hope of rescue? I couldn't leave like this. I waited in the blackness for him to return, but he was gone, leaving me with conflicting emotions and guilt. I stole back into the gutter feeling as if I'd given away my two most precious possessions, a wife in love with a younger, braver, more exciting man, and my child, the sole reason for my remaining on this planet of war, flame, and torment. My hands were shaking, so I placed them in my coat pocket. I felt Rosenfeld's pipe bowl. My mind was snapping from all I'd lost, was losing, might lose.

I skirted past Balut Square. I could visualize still the man hanging from the gallows, swinging before our dead eyes. Were German police staring balefully from their headquarters? I thought how easy it would be to provoke one bullet. One explosion of pain and this suffering would be over. I held back the tears for my lost friend. The deportations now had a face to them. I prayed the old Professor was safe in a new home, somewhere in the farmlands of Poland. I suspected I'd never find out what happened to him, at least until the war was over. Jews disappeared and were never heard from again. I cupped the bowl of my friend's pipe and swore that with God's help, someday, Miriam and I would enjoy dinner with Rosenfeld and his beloved, Rosa. Miriam and Regina would love the old man. They would laugh when I told them the story of how I stole gloves from a dead body to keep his hands warm.

CHAPTER 21

M AY 21, 1942:
  LARGE ORDERS
  are constantly being placed here in the ghetto. I have
learned from reliable sources that the dry cleaners have received consecutive
consignments of 300 train cars of dirty underclothes for cleaning...The
woodwork factory, apart from its current orders, is to produce a million
pairs of clogs. 800 people work there in three shifts. The metal workshop is
supposed to have work enough for two years. ... BO

I had taken to signing a few of my entries. I suppose I wanted
to distinguish them from the articulate writing of the others, take
ownership of my meager contributions. I wanted the future to know
I existed...we existed. Singer had frightened me, reaffirming that
we were all walking on the thinnest of ice. The new work orders
from the military were reassuring, after all, why would we be getting
such orders if the authorities planned to shut us down? Two plus
two equals four, even for the Germans. I wondered if I should
relate this information to Singer, ask him to delay whatever he was
contemplating to rescue Miriam and my Regina.

Heilig entered. He was shaking. "Ostrowski, it was heart-breaking."
He held his pencil like a dagger. "I saw the women from Pabianice,
the ones who lost their children."

"You went there?" Didn't he realize how dangerous that was? He
had no family, no real friends. He could afford the risk.

"Everyone should see this for themselves."

"I've seen enough misery to last a lifetime." If only I could confide in him, in anyone.

Heilig's eyes were staring at me. "Anyone with children should see this."

"I don't want to know more. Have you seen the Germans are demanding more work from us?" I attempted to steer him away. "Just look at all these requisitions." I handed him my report.

He skimmed through it and then gazed into my eyes as if he understood my motive for sharing this news.

I was clutching at straws, as if at a life ring. "With all this work they need, they must keep our factories going. Why would they order so much if they intend to shut us down?"

Heilig gave a weak smile. "Of course, you are right. Why would they place such massive orders if they plan to dismantle the ghetto?"

"I'm right, aren't I?" I wanted his reassurance. I needed it.

"Yes. Of course, you're right."

I felt some relief. Maybe the next time Singer contacted me, I would tell him I'd reconsidered. There was no reason to risk his life. We'd wait out the war right here. With all these orders, we were safe.

Heilig kept working, but abruptly muttered, "You did say truckloads of dirty underwear?"

I pulled out what I'd written, what I'd signed. There it was. How did I gloss over that? I searched for the report from the drycleaning director. Men's, women's, children's...truckloads of dirty underwear...all mixed in...no way to return them to the owners.

Cukier entered the room. "No sign of the Professor still?"

I didn't want to be the one to tell him. I suspected he knew Rosenfeld's fate already. I rose from my chair. "I'll be back later," I said.

Cukier didn't bother asking where I was off to. We had formed a solid bond, and he was more a brother now than my boss. "Be safe, my friend," he said and began the daily burrowing into the mounting piles of memoranda and departmental reports.

I almost turned back, but Heilig's eyes urged me on.

German soldiers sneered as I picked my way past them in the hallway. I clutched my papers. I knew the risk I was taking.

The streets were eerily empty. I walked with authority, just in case. I expected to be stopped, but the Jewish police glanced at my papers held high in front of me and waved me on. Had they lost interest too?

I really didn't want to see the place for myself, but it had drawn me to it like a magnet. Before I placed Miriam and Regina...Singer, into danger, I had to learn the truth.

Two Jewish policemen guarded the door. One examined my identification. "Administrator," he said, and waved me past.

I knew where the building was. It didn't take me long to get there. The hour I spent within its cursed chamber was one of the longest in my life.

The others were still at lunch in Kitchen 2 when I returned to our office. I was glad to have the room for myself. I needed time. I sat down in our workroom and cried. I hated this tight space, the long table and chairs making it almost impossible to walk around, but it was safe...for now. After what I'd witnessed, no, experienced, it seemed a sanctuary. Unable to scream, not wanting to cry because my friends might return at any moment, I forced myself to write.

When Heilig and Cukier returned, I handed the Weasel my report. "Please, read it aloud," I said. I wasn't able.

Heilig began to read in his monotone voice. "Nothing could be more shocking than to visit the site at 22 Masarska Street where over a thousand women from Pabianice have been quartered." He looked over the paper at me.

"You went there?" Cukier had a worried expression on his face.

I nodded.

"You shouldn't have," Cukier said, holding the filthy handkerchief in front of his mouth.

"I had to."

Heilig continued, "In every room, in every corner, one sees mothers,

111

sisters, grandmothers shaken by sobs, quietly lamenting the loss of their little children. All children up to age 10 have been sent off to parts unknown."

I gripped my seat. Here, I'd felt reassured by the factory orders, but Heilig reading my entry shot all that to hell. I wished he'd stop reading, but had to hear the words I'd written or I might lose my resolve.

Heilig bit his upper lip. "Some of these sad women have lost three, four, even six children. Their quiet despair is profoundly penetrating, so different from the loud laments we are accustomed to hearing at deaths and funerals, but all the more real and sincere for all that. It is no surprise that anyone with small children or old parents awaits the days to come with trepidation—"

"Stop," I said, my voice cracking.

"This is good writing," Heilig said.

Cukier was silent.

"It is the truth." I aimed that at Julian. "Okay, you may finish now."

Heilig nodded. "The greatest optimists have lost hope. Until now, people had thought that work would maintain the ghetto and the majority of people without any breakup of families. Now it is clear that even this was an illusion." He looked at me and then continued, "There were plenty of orders in Pabianice and Brzesiny, but that did not protect the Jews against wholesale deportation."

I glanced at Julian.

He was deep in thought and then said softly, "You surprise me."

"In what way?"

"I have not seen you reveal emotions before." He sucked in his lips. "It is very good. Heilig is right, but you are missing one thing."

"What is that?"

"I would add, "Our last hope is our Chairman: people believe that he will succeed.""

"You still believe that?" I was starving for hope, hope of any kind.

Cukier nodded.

I took back the sheet and added, "Our last hope is our Chairman:

people believe that he will succeed, if not totally, then at least in part, in averting the calamities that now loom ahead." I wasn't sure I believed that anymore, but it was all that might get my entry included. I handed it to Julian.

"I noticed you signed it?"

"I don't want anyone else to take the blame." I handed the entry to Cukier.

Our leader reread it and said, "I'm going home. Our great writer is in charge." He looked like an old man as he helped himself to his feet with the support of the table. "Yes, it is well written."

"Good-bye, Julian." After Rosenfeld's disappearance, I could not take it for granted that we would ever see each other again. I would never be able to take a salutation for granted either.

"God bless you, Engineer," he replied, giving me a smile. "You'll see, all will be well."

"God bless you," I said, as the door revealed Gestapo officers standing next to several Jewish policemen. Were they staring at our door?

CHAPTER 22

SUNDAY, MAY 25, 1942: *TRAMLINE INTRODUCED*
Now under discussion is a project to introduce a tramline in the ghetto that would run first to Marysin, where many workshops are located.

I was waiting anxiously for word from Singer. The faces I'd seen in that holding tank were indelible memories, as were the sobs, the wailing of the mothers, whose arms ached, empty without their children. The images haunted me. Where was he? What was taking so long to plan an escape?

As I sat in my chair, Miriam lay a bombshell at my feet. It came from nowhere, the end of our desperate attempts to pretend we were still a couple. I had just walked up the stairs, never sure what was awaiting me: a summons from the Resettlement Commission, a visit from the German soldiers, a battle with Miriam. I bent to kiss her forehead, something I forced myself to do. Duty complete, I faced the empty wood chair as if it was hooked up to electric wires. That's when the bomb hit.

"I'm going to work," Miriam said. "I've arranged for Dorka Wasserstein to watch over Regina. She loves children and—"

"No, you are not," I shouted, halting in my descent to the chair. "Regina needs you home. End of discussion."

She glared at me but dropped the discussion…at least until the next night.

"I've gotten a job," she said as if stating a mathematical fact.

"I told you, no job."

Miriam crossed her arms over her chest. "I need to get out of this flat. I'm going insane." She looked as if she was about to cry and scream at the same time.

"Regina needs you," I replied, convinced I was right.

"I'll be home early. It is part-time work."

"No."

"Please? I need a few hours to keep going. It is not far. I will be home early."

"It doesn't matter. I don't want you out there. It isn't safe."

"Nowhere is safe. A small job will not hurt me. You said yourself the enemy are not taking people who are working."

I was about to launch an attack, but she was right about that That was the strategy on which the Chairman based our survival. I studied my wife, her stubborn expression, those angry eyes. "Let's discuss this calmly—"

"That's the problem. You believe everything is subject to the laws of mathematics and logic. When I said I wanted to get the hell out of Poland, you refused, but look what is happening. You've heard of the women sent here without their children? I know you have. You thought you could keep that from me?"

I shifted uneasily in my seat. "I did not want to upset you more than you already are." I sounded spineless. "You are not leaving our child and taking on some job."

Miriam walked toward me, a stern look on her face. "Let's say, for one instant, you are right, and I've been wrong. Let's say the Chairman is the only way out of this mess we are in. My taking a job in his new warehouse may be just enough to buy us time." She gave me a meaningful look. "I've made up my mind. End of discussion."

But it wasn't. I argued for two days, my blood boiling, but it was no use. Nothing I brought up made my obstinate wife change her mind. I finally asked, "What kind of job is it?" I hoped I might still poke holes in her insane desire to work.

115

"It's in the old warehouse, a few blocks from here. I'm not sure what I'll be doing, but I've been told there is lots of work coming in all the time." She glanced lovingly at Regina who was on the floor hugging her rag doll. "I believe it is a clothing factory. There were lots of trucks, and I saw bags and bags stacked up inside. Maybe I can pick up a few bits for Regina."

I wondered if I told her about my meeting with Singer if that would stem her obsession to get a job. But what if nothing came of his search for an escape plan? I didn't know if she could bear another disappointment. Could I? "I still don't like leaving Regina with anyone. I'm tired of arguing with you. I wish you'd change your mind, but if you are resolute—"

"You'll see. It will make a new me. I've been cooped up in here too long." She cracked a smile. "Dorka used to be a teacher. She will teach Regina what she needs to know when schools open again."

"One thing. If anyone has typhus, you will promise to quit." I'd heard the newcomers had brought typhus with them. "That is non-negotiable."

"Agreed."

I watched Miriam pick up our almost one-year-old child. Her arms were thin, hardly enough muscle to lift the small wriggling bundle. "Things will be better. You'll see," she said, holding Regina against her chest. "Mommy will be happy again."

The decision made, accepting defeat to end the confrontations, I felt like a deflated balloon. It calmed me gradually to see my two girls playing. There were few playthings, so they made do with silly clapping games and songs that reminded me of my childhood long ago. The lull was deceptive.

It wasn't until later that night, sleepless in our bed, that I thought I heard the pitiful weeping of the mothers from Pabianice.

CHAPTER 23

FRIDAY, MAY 28, 1942: *AN ATROCIOUS FRAUD*
After a preliminary investigation, the Order Service arrested an unlicensed manufacturer of 'salad' produced from scraps retrieved from the garbage. This item, whose deceptive appearance was similar to the popular community salads, consisted of rotting matter in the final stages of decay and was primarily sold to newcomers in unlawful transactions. Two families numbering about a dozen people were arrested.

"Incredible," Cukier said. "For every problem the Nazis load on us, there is a criminal element eager to make it worse. Thank God the Chairman and the Order Service stopped them from selling their poison."

Heilig was muttering as he read an official looking document. "What do you think this means?" he asked. "On Thursday, the Chairman ordered the elimination of the public kitchens as of June 1."

"No more soup kitchens?" Each day the lines grew longer and more restive, but how would people survive without the kitchens?

Cukier said, "It doesn't include kitchen 2."

"But there were more than 50 kitchens." I dug through the files. "They served over 40,000 workers and about 10,000 of the newcomers! What will happen to them? How will they get food? What about the almost 2,000 kitchen workers? You know what it means if they have no jobs."

"I don't know anything about this," Cukier said. "Let's move on."

Heilig was still reading the original report. "The Chairman gave a speech Thursday afternoon, as usual." He laughed but stopped when he saw Cukier's sharp look. "He announced all employees, in all probability, will receive an additional 150 grams of bread in the place of the soup and 40 grams of sausage."

Cukier sighed. "I suppose everyone will be racking their brains on this most pressing question: which is better, a plate of soup, or a piece of bread and sausage." He burst into a fit of coughing. "Let's move on, I said. It seems our stack of mail is growing deeper each day." He glanced at Rosenfeld's vacant chair. "We need more help."

Neither of us mentioned our old friend, Doctor Rosenfeld, nor Singer, but I think we both knew neither were coming back.

Heilig read another notice. "On Wednesday, there was a concert performed by the symphony orchestra."

Cukier said, "I would have attended, but my coughing would have disturbed the others. I love listening to Miss Rotsztat, with her beautiful violin performances. I miss that."

Heilig muttered, "Insanity."

Cukier laughed and said, "So, what else is new? We're all insane here." He burst into a series of coughs, but couldn't find his handkerchief. He finally found it, marred with black and red streaks, in his trouser pocket.

I no longer mentioned the concerts to Miriam predicting how she would react. Like many other things I kept to myself, concerts for the elite, while everyone else was suffering would be another wedge between us.

The door opened, and I sprang to attention. The Germans were everywhere and our small chamber, hidden though it was, in the rear of the Department of the Archives, was frequently inspected. It could be invaded at any time.

Neftalin hurried in. "I wanted to deliver this myself. I've been the bearer of too much bad news of late." He held a cardboard rectangle in his hand. "Today, we received this card from a resident of the ghetto who was sent to a labor camp near Poznan on May 15 of this year."

Why was this good news? Cukier was coughing, unable to rise from his chair, so I reached for the card. "It is stamped Poznan, May 23, 1942," I said, examining the postcard. "It's in German. Heilig, can you translate it? My German isn't good enough."

Heilig took the card gingerly as if afraid it might crumble. "*To the Eldest of the Jews of the Litzmannstadt Ghetto. Please forward this card to my sister, Bronka Dab, 28 Zgierska Street for which I thank you. –Nachman Dab.*" He paused. "Does anyone know him?"

None of us did.

Heilig continued, "*My dear sister, Bronka. I am writing you a few words just after arriving in the camp. I am well and satisfied that I have gone to do manual labor. I am working very hard at laying concrete, and I eat three times a day.*" He glanced at me. "Three meals? I wish we were so blessed."

Cukier smiled. "This is the first card we have gotten from a deportee to this camp. It is good news."

I'd become Singer, the resident skeptic. I'd hold my judgment until all the evidence was in.

Heilig continued translating, "*I get two good soups and bread. Other than that, there's nothing new. Next time, I will write you more, but now I am tired from my trip.*" He looked up again and smiled before he read aloud, "*I kiss you and send my regards. Your brother.*" He turned over the card. "On this side, he jotted down a few words to his girlfriend, telling her he's not hungry. That's it."

I fell back in my chair. We finally had some correspondence from a deportee. One postcard did not erase all my suspicions. How could it? But it reignited hope that soon we would hear more about the fate of our resettled people, especially the children. "What is the postmark?" I asked, still suspicious.

Heilig looked. "Gemeinschaftslager D.A.F."

Neftalin smiled. "That is the camp's address."

Cukier said, "It seems genuine...addressed to his sister. He knew her name. Yes, it seems genuine."

"Of course, it is," Neftalin said. "Many people saw it already. Everyone says it is real. He even writes to his girlfriend. Gentlemen, it is our first sign of hope. I could not wait to share it with you, my good friends."

One card, as much as I wished it, was not enough to dispel my fears over the fate of our deportees. It offered hope more cards would soon arrive. I reasoned the authorities had kept the mail from us, for some unknown purpose, and now, perhaps because we had been so 'well-behaved,' they were allowing some mail to trickle through. At any rate, this small glimmer I intended to share with Miriam. I hoped it would crack through her depression.

Heilig was reading more entries. "The world is ending," he announced with a grand flourish, obviously in a better mood after reading the postcard.

"What now?" Cukier asked. "Why must you always be so dramatic?"

Heilig laughed. "Someone will be happy today. A new shipment of army denims, which were to be sent to the Brzesniny factories for tailoring, has arrived here. More work for everyone means the ghetto is safe."

Cukier laughed. "You see, the Chairman was right! The Germans would not send us all these uniforms if they were going to throw us all out of our beloved ghetto."

"But what happened to Brzesniny?" I asked.

Cukier said, "It's gone."

I knew better than to question him.

"They are trucking in dozens of sewing machines," Heilig announced. "More good omens."

"Sewing machines?" In the unexpected cascade of good news, I'd forgotten about Singer. Had he tried that dangerous ploy again? With all this hopeful news, did I want to risk escaping from the ghetto? What was on the outside for escaped Jews? Sealed in as we were, almost nothing got to us from the outside world. The devil you know is better than the devil you don't. "Where are the sewing machines now?" I had to get to Singer before he did anything rash.

"Why such interest in sewing machines?" Cukier asked but was overcome by another of his frequent coughing fits.

I glanced at Heilig, but he showed no clue that he grasped my reason for asking about the sewing machines. Was he ignorant or a good actor? One way or the other, I would find out.

CHAPTER 24

MAY 31, 1942: INSPECTION OF THE GHETTO
On Saturday, the mayor of Litzmannstadt, Werner Ventzki, inspected the ghetto accompanied by a number of people both in uniform and in civilian clothes. The representatives inspected a series of workshops and took photographs.

Cukier asked, "Engineer, how many of these inspections by Germans do you have recorded?"

I jumped when he called on me. My mind was focused on Miriam, specifically about a discussion we'd had last night. I'd been in a more optimistic mood and didn't notice that her initial elation about working had quickly faded. She had not been open with me for a long time. There were secrets we both harbored that made candor almost impossible. So, I was alarmed when after Regina was asleep, Miriam stood over me, nervous about something.

"May I talk to you?" She asked, checking to see if the baby was asleep.

"Of course." I thought of the shipment of sewing machines. Had Singer contacted her? Had he made her an offer I could never match? I couldn't read her face. "What is it?" I sounded irritated, too terse. "Please, tell me? I'll try and help."

Miriam spoke hesitantly. "I was okay with my little job. I was sweeping the offices. Then they moved me to a warehouse to clean. Not far...Brzezinzska Street...number 75. I was fine, working hard. It was exercise and fresh air. A change."

I pictured my wife sweeping out a warehouse floor. That alone made me bristle with anger, but it had been her choice to go back to work. If this was her problem, it was her own fault. "Do you want to quit now? Is that it?" I'd thought of giving up my depressing job numerous times, but that would be an automatic ticket to the unknown fate of the deportees for Miriam and Regina. I no longer counted in the equation. "I don't know if you can quit once you are working for the Chairman," I said, trying to sound sympathetic.

"No. Please, listen?" Miriam waited until sure I was attentive. "I didn't mind the cleaning, even of toilets, but then the trucks arrived. They came in groups. They were very large…lots of them."

"Trucks carry things to warehouses," I said.

Miriam looked frightened.

"Miriam, you don't have to be afraid. Just tell me what you saw." I reached for her hand. She didn't pull it away. "They rushed us all to the loading area. The Order Service men shouted at us, ordered us to unload the trucks. At first, I was uncaring of what the cargo was. Much of the material was wrapped in improvised sacks…tied rugs, blankets, sheets. I thought it was bedding from the military, a hospital or hotel. Some of the bundles were different…"

"How were they different?"

Miriam brushed her hand back through her hair. "Bennie, they were shirts and slips rolled together, three or four at a time. We were throwing things so fast that I didn't think much about the contents, but there were pants, rolled up with pairs of unmentionables inside the rolls. I was curious but too busy to take in much detail. When some coats and jackets were put in my arms, I saw…"

"What did you see?"

Miriam's voice lowered, "All had been ripped at the seams, pockets torn…"

Oh, God. I kept it in. My poor wife. If she was right… I shivered. I remembered the Chairman had established a Department of Used Articles and had designated five vacant warehouses for storage.

Singer's report. "Miriam, it is vitally important you tell me the rest," I said, trying to keep my voice from revealing what I feared.

Miriam peered into my eyes. She reminded me of a frightened kitten. "Do you know what it means? I was stumped. It slowly came to me, but I didn't believe it. It was too horrible to accept. They moved me to another truck. There were thousands of prayer shawls..."

"Prayer shawls?"

"Yes. Thousands. Not new."

"What else?"

Miriam squeezed my hand. "As we unloaded the trucks, the police watched us like hawks. They scooped up certain items that fell: papers...letters...ID cards..." She shivered. "Bennie, what does it mean?" That frightened cat look again, eyes searching me.

I was a sucker for that vulnerable look. I pulled Miriam against me, feeling her tremble. She had not let me hold her like that for months. If she was crying, she was stifling it, perhaps not wishing to wake Regina. I didn't tell her what I suspected. I couldn't share what I believed was the horror story taking place somewhere in our tortured land. How could I share with her, a child herself, weeping against me, desperate for some other explanation, my suspicions? How could I reveal where I thought all these items had come from? My theory was too incredible for me to believe, to accept. There had to be another explanation. Perhaps, they were from shuttered factories? Yes, that could be it. Rolled pants with unmentionables—I almost laughed at the term Miriam had used—a factory would never wrap underwear in rolled pants. Would they? Dirty linens from hospitals? Too many. Trucks and trucks of used clothing... "Miriam, the papers and I.D. cards...did you see names, any addresses?"

Still pressed against me, she said, "They scooped them up almost as soon as we picked them up from the floor. I spotted some were from other cities in Poland. A few from here. They fell from the bundles. I wanted to keep one to show you. I was afraid. I'm sorry."

"You have nothing to be sorry about. You were right not to chance it." I shivered at the thought of her being arrested for concealing one of the ID cards. But God, I would have liked to see one. "You know you have to go back," I said, after several minutes of holding her trembling body in silence.

"I don't want to."

I felt like shouting at her that I had warned her not to go to work for the Chairman, but this was not the time to gloat or say, "I told you so." All I could do was rock her against me. I felt as if I were a father rocking a stubborn, recalcitrant, child, who had acknowledged her helplessness in the face of a horrifying discovery. "I know, but you must…at least, for now." I would find Singer and speed things up. I didn't know how long Miriam's brain could take working with this nightmare buzzing inside. "I know you are thinking the worst possible scenario," I said, choosing my words carefully, "but there are other explanations possible."

"Bennie, you should see the trucks. There are so many. What other explanation is there? All the used clothing…"

"They may come from anywhere…hospitals, hotels, other ghettos closed down to move the populace away from the war. The world is closing in on Hitler by now. It can't go on much longer. It just can't."

Miriam mumbled something.

"I'm sorry. What did you say?"

"I saw lots of children's clothes…baby clothes."

I felt her shiver again. I could think of nothing to say that would comfort her. I rocked her silently in the darkness of our flat, wishing the night would be abruptly blasted by the sound of airplanes dropping bombs on our damn factories.

"Do you want to go to bed?" Miriam asked after I thought she was asleep. She didn't wait for my answer but lifted away from me.

I wasn't sure I'd heard right, so I remained seated until I felt her hand leading me. Blinded, exhausted, I let her guide me to the bed and pull me fully clothed onto the shabby mattress. I was frightened she wanted to make love. I wasn't sure I was capable of that anymore, not tonight. I was grateful when she pulled me to her bosom and held my head tightly against her. Would I weep? I didn't want to. I had to be strong for her.

"I'm sorry," Miriam said several times.

I was the one who should have apologized to her. It was my fault we were still here. It was right that she didn't love me. I didn't deserve it. When I felt her hand reaching down for me, I moved it away. "You don't have to—"

"I want to," she whispered and lowered her hand again.

I pulled my face from her breasts and stared into her eyes. It was as if I was asking her if she knew it was me, and not my young rival. I felt her urging me toward her and gave in, eager to accept whatever gift she was willing to bestow on my unworthy body. It did not take long before I moved over her, her breasts covered in that filthy chemise, her eyes closed…perhaps she did not want to see me. "Please, open your eyes," I said. "I need you to open your eyes." When she opened them, there was a smile on her face. Yes, she knew it was me.

For one night, the clock was set back to a time when there was no war, no despair…no Singer. For a few minutes, there was only Miriam and me, our bodies working to revive from each other's exhausted shells whatever passion was left. As we held each other, I prayed that our love-making did not waken our beautiful child.

When Miriam slept, I lay awake, listening to Regina breathing. Such fleeting joy in a dark world. And then, I saw again the trucks filled with soiled clothing.

CHAPTER 25

J UNE 1, 1942
104,469 people were living in the ghetto. The month of May was marked by a difficult food supply situation.

I left before Miriam awoke. I wanted to run but had enough awareness that I knew it could be fatal. There were too many German police showing up at inopportune times. What Miriam revealed stuck in my brain like a dagger that would not dislodge. Heilig had to help me get to Singer. I would arrive early and use every bit of intimidation left in my body to get him to relay to Singer my urgent message.

Unfortunately, Heilig was late. Cukier was late. I was alone with piles of notes and memoranda that seemed even more pointless than usual. The population was decreasing at an alarming rate, but then I noted, 7,000 Jews had been dumped here in May. The Germans were using as some kind of holding tank. They were moving Jews like chess pieces, first into the ghetto, and then out. But to where? Why?

Employment figures had risen dramatically. I recalled the Chairman's slogan, "Everyone in the ghetto must work, for only work can assure our survival." Whole families registered for work, from 10-year-old children to grey-haired old people. They were beating on the doors of the Bureau of Labor to get assigned somewhere, anywhere. They had become believers in Rumkowski's theory, but how could he manage to employ everyone?

Cukier entered leaning on his walking stick. "You're here early," he said, glancing at the stacks of paper on our table. "I'm going to ask for help."

"There are plenty who would want this job. Crowds of people are screaming to register for work now," I said. "It's a zoo."

Cukier frowned. "It's because of the Medical Commission last month."

"You may be right." Fear spread when a group of German doctors, accompanied by Gestapo, conducted medical examinations. Everyone wondered what the Latin letters stamped even on long-time ghetto residents meant.

"As long as we are working, we should be safe," Cukier said. "Your Miriam is working now?"

I nodded. Should I report what Miriam had related to me?

"Food prices are sky-high. A loaf of bread is 600 marks! We'll have to fight the roaches for every valuable crumb. Shit, the roaches are stronger than we are." Cukier coughed into his nose rag.

Heilig burst into the room. "All the public kitchens are closed except four. The vegetable distribution points are closed too."

Cukier laughed. "What good would they be with no vegetables?"

Heilig said, "This is no laughing matter. There was such a demand for potato peels that people were forging doctor certificates. So now they've stopped all distribution of even potato peels. Are the Nazis trying to starve us to death?"

Cukier shook his head. "The Chairman is working to halt the inflation of prices. I heard him speak on the 23rd of this month. He hadn't made a speech for some time. It was a good speech. I think it assured many people—"

"Did he mention the resettlements?" I interrupted.

Cukier looked uncertain. "Yes. He briefly discussed the resettlement of about 55,000 people."

"55,000 more?" I couldn't take it in. What the hell was going on?

Cukier's face hardened. "He screamed that much of the blame is ours since so many refused to work. He reminded everyone he had warned of the need to register, to work, and the consequences. He repeated this at every possible opportunity. There is no excuse for people not registering. It is their own damn fault." He fell into another fit of coughing.

Cukier was right that the Chairman had hammered that point over and over to us. Only fools would have ignored his warnings.

Cukier was breathing heavily. "There was a major difference in this latest speech." He took several deep breaths. "He said it softly, but I heard it like thunder." He let out a deep breath and said, "The Eldest of the Jews said, "selecting those to be resettled had been taken out of his hands.""

"He admitted that in public?"

Cukier nodded. "But he also said he managed to keep 30,000 in the ghetto who registered for work but were not yet employed. He is working on new jobs daily. In fact, he is creating a workshop with "easy work" for children over 10. He is also laying in plans for a new train line, providing more jobs and public transportation within the ghetto."

"I wonder why we need a new train line?" Heilig asked.

"It will create many new jobs. That is his objective." Cukier said. "Here's another new order for the army. The tailoring factory will suspend all work on civilian clothes and work exclusively for the army from now on." Cukier gave me the order. "That is hopeful."

I did not love the idea that we were manufacturing goods for the Nazis, but thus far, based on rumors of what had happened to the other ghettos, the Chairman's strategy was successful. Our work for the German military might be all saving us from the fate of Jews all over Europe.

Heilig held up another report. "Here's something. Hundreds of sewing machines have been supplied to the saddlery and tailor shops." He laughed. "We'll all soon have to learn to sew."

My ears perked up. "Does it say where the machines came from?" Singer had hidden in such a shipment before.

Heilig gave me a curious look. "No. Just that they were not in boxes.

I assume they've been used."

Would Singer use the same ploy again?

"Used sewing machines? Where would they be from?" Heilig muttered.

"Have any of you heard of the Chairman's new warehouses?" I could not keep this to myself any longer.

Heilig asked, "Why are you asking about warehouses?"

Cukier handed me a memo. "I received this from an unnamed Order Service man a few days ago. He reported four five-ton trucks were brought to the warehouse at the saddlery. The shipments came from Brzesiny. He claimed the trucks were full of footwear. They were under heavy guard by the Germans. Or so, he said."

Heilig looked puzzled. "Why are shoes being heavily guarded?"

Cukier said, "The policeman said he was surprised to see the heels and soles on the shoes were missing. It was as if all had been torn off."

"Torn off?" Heilig still looked puzzled.

Cukier nodded. "There were thousands of shoes... men's, women's...children's." He closed his eyes.

Oh, God. I visualized a room stacked from floor to ceiling with used shoes, all with missing soles and heels. Men's, women's, children's shoes. I'd never seen such a terrifying image.

CHAPTER 26

T HURSDAY, JUNE 4, 1942
    At midnight, on Sunday, a woman whose personal data has not
    been established was shot to death in the immediate vicinity of the
barbed wire on Drukarska Street. On Monday at 4:30 A.M. a man was
shot and killed on the roadway, having first passed through the barbed wire.
The incident took place at the building at 56 Zgierska Street.

Each time I read of a shooting, or an arrest, at the barbed wire, I held
my breath. Please, God, don't let it be Singer?" I felt guilty begging
him to find some way to rescue Miriam and Regina. I knew he was
risking his life, but the more I thought about the used clothing and
shoes trucked into the warehouses, the more frightened I felt about
the noose tightening around us.

With my Administrator I.D., I thought of venturing into a warehouse
to see for myself what was being stored there. I still didn't believe
the reports. But did I really want to see children's soiled underthings
and shoes with missing heels and soles? Two and two make four.
I suspected the Germans tore off the heels and soles searching for
the few precious coins, bills, or jewels, deceased people had tried
to conceal. And yes, I now believed that all these items were from
people who were either imprisoned or dead. But it was impossible to
conceive. What could kill so many people?

Miriam had said she saw thousands of taleisim,(tal-a-sim), prayer
shawls. She saw stains and filth on some of these holy garments. It was
impossible for me, an engineer, to envision how so many men could

131

be killed in such a short period. I had no explanation, just growing fear and puzzlement of how such a massive execution, a genocide, was possible. The magnitude of such a mass murder made me doubt that anyone, not even Hitler, could accomplish such a depraved feat. But how could I account for the growing mounds of evidence?

Cukier stumbled into the room. He was coughing hard.

I did not know how he managed to come here each day. I suspected, after Rosenfeld's disappearance, and Singer's, that he did not want to risk being labeled too sick to work. As I saw him drag himself around the table, I dreaded one day seeing his chair empty. He was my last friend from our original crew.

"Good morning, Engineer," Cukier said, wiping his mouth with his always-present rag. "I barely made it past a long line at the tobacco kiosks. Apparently, there's been a great drop in price." He let out a blistering series of coughs. "I guess the Nazis want to kill us all with smoking." He laughed but burst into coughing again. "What's the news?"

"There was another shooting on Zgierska," I said. "On Monday, at about 4:30. They didn't list the name."

Cukier searched his files. "It was a woman. No identity. Shot to death. Wait. Yes, they also killed a man. Perhaps Heilig has the report in his files already?"

I hated not knowing. What if it was Singer? It would be a terrible blow to our hope for escape. I could hear Miriam crying when she found out. But would we find out? When Rosenfeld disappeared, it was as if he never existed, no explanation. I couldn't risk asking the officials who handled resettlements. The wrong question, and off I'd go into the unknown. I felt for the pipe bowl in my pocket. It was still there. If the sentries killed me, they would never figure out why something so useless was in my possession. I reached into Heilig's files. "It's unending," I said, flipping through to see if any were from the police precinct where the incident occurred.

Cukier asked, "Why are you so interested shootings lately? You are usually concerned with the statistics only."

I didn't want to tell him that if the victim was Singer, it was my fault. "I'm just curious why we don't have the victims' personal information for our entries."

Cukier interrupted, "There's something going on. I saw unusual detachments of police at the entry point today. Have you noticed many workers were out early this morning cleaning streets?"

"No. What's happening now?"

Cukier leaned closer.

Did I smell blood? I backed away slightly.

Cukier said, "I went to our friend, Neftalin. He said ten cars arrived bearing among others, Gauleiter Greiser and minister Schwarz, the Nazi party treasurer. The Chairman himself met them at the gate and escorted them around the ghetto."

"That's why no children are around," Heilig said.

"No infirm or elderly either. The Chairman wants the ghetto to look like a labor camp, where nobody is seen as idle." Cukier coughed into his rag and then continued. "Neftalin informed me this is not an ordinary inspection, but may concern the ghetto's very existence—"

"Any clue how it went?" Neftalin's admission surprised me.

"From what I've heard the Germans appeared satisfied. Let us pray it is so." Cukier closed his eyes. "God, all we want is to be left in peace. Let the occupiers recognize our labor as vital to their effort."

Heilig shook his head.

God, I prayed silently, please let Singer find a way to get us free from this hell-hole?

Miriam was smiling when I returned home. "We were given a gift of a supplementary ration of sweets," she said, showing off a tiny parcel of sugar.

"Who gave that to you?" I was suspicious. Lately, she looked better. I thought it was to prepare for her job, but now I wondered. When she smiled, she reminded me of the lovely girl I fell in love with before this nightmare began...before she betrayed me.

Miriam laughed. "Oh, Gina, your daddy is so funny." She gave the child a grin. "It is a gift from the Chairman for the positive impression the workers made today on the authorities."

"Did you see the Nazi officials?" I asked.

"No, but I saw the parade of cars. They made us stand in the street as they went by. There were fine black motorcars and behind came the Chairman's coach. His horse looks as if it is on his last legs. He had the chief of the Order Service with him, and they were followed by a truck full of German policemen. The Jewish police walked along the sides of the convoy. It was quite a parade."

"What did the Chairman's face look like? Was he smiling?"

"He looked straight ahead. I would say he did not look happy. No." She frowned. "But the news must have been good for him to give us little gifts."

The problem was that we never knew what was happening. We were in suspense. No control over our fate. We were riders on an ocean wave, never sure if it would lift us up or send us screaming in terror, crushing our bones with brutal force. It was time for another lie: "Yes, I'm guessing the news must have been good." Was it? The Germans had toured their possessions in impressive automobiles while the Eldest of the Jews, in whose hands we entrusted our lives, followed in a dilapidated coach, dragged by a broken-down horse.

Back at work the following morning, I was relieved to learn that the man shot by the sentries wasn't Singer. A police report only identified him as a nineteen-year-old, who, like many others who met death at the barbed wire, had been "retarded."

Singer's fate was still unknown.

CHAPTER 27

T HURSDAY, JUNE 11, 1942: *FILMING*
In the last few days considerable filming has been done in the ghetto...they filmed outside in the streets and inside in workshops, institutions and hospitals. Among other things, a circumcision ceremony was filmed in Hospital No. 1.

Each morning, if we were alone, I asked Heilig the same question, and he replied the same: "No, I have not seen him. I have not heard from him. I don't know anyone who has." I felt like punching him in the face but suspected he was too afraid of me not to tell the truth.

As desperate as I was to find Singer and launch an escape, things in the ghetto had improved. Circulars announced a special food allocation for all working people. We were hopeful again.

Even Miriam was excited. "Look Benny, potatoes, margarine, white sugar, 100 rye flakes, ersatz coffee, and even 100 grams of marmalade to every employee. I'm so glad I insisted on working, aren't you?"

"You were right all along." I was glad she was no longer upset by the flow of used clothing into the warehouses. Food, after one is starving, has a way of making us forget. The taste of marmalade after so long, of coffee...artificial, yes, but with a little sugar, it was passable. It was easy to believe the worst was behind us.

I was thinking of Miriam's face, lips glossy with marmalade, when the door opened.

I expected Cukier.

"What do you do in here?" A German in a black uniform asked.

I leaped to attention, fear shooting through me.

Another German entered the room. He was aiming something at me. A camera?

"I said what do you do here?" The first German official repeated, the camera whirring behind him.

Neftalin entered, hair slicked back, suit and tie perfectly matched, leather laced shoes highly polished. He replied in German. "These are our record keepers. We keep the Chairman's files here, so they are available in one place for you."

The German leaned forward, reading my notes on the typewriter. "These are in Polish. I do not read Polish."

Neftalin looked uneasy. "We can do them in German from now on."

The German looked at me, his eyes hostile. "Sprechen zie Deutch?"

"Yavul, Mein Herr." I hoped he wasn't going to test me. I was too nervous.

"There is nothing here." The official signaled the cameraman to stop filming. "Is this work important? They produce nothing for us here."

A chill shot through me.

Neftalin grabbed a sheet of paper from my pile. "The numbers here are records of how many uniforms we have made for your great army. And here are the number and sizes of shoes. It is all very organized. Without these men keeping all documents centrally located, our efficiency would plummet, and the military's costs would skyrocket."

The German sneered. "This is very boring. Let us film elsewhere." He gave Cukier a hawkish look. "Is that Jew ill?"

Cukier dropped the handkerchief to his lap. "Nein, Herr Oberfuhrer, I am suffering from an allergy. That is all."

The officer studied Cukier for a long moment, waved his hand, and the cameraman backed out of the room.

Neftalin quickly followed.

Almost instantly, Cukier broke down into a body-wracking fit of coughing.

Heilig looked like he was going to faint.

I kept staring at the door, waiting for it to burst open, armed Gestapo rushing toward us with rifle butts aimed at our heads.

When, after a short while, the monsters did not reappear, we breathed a sigh of relief and returned to our work. Silently, we sifted through the mail, setting aside a few items from the departmental reports. Will this never end? I listed more suicides and thanked the Chairman for providing me this job, this protection from whatever fate awaited those unfortunates who were no longer within our walls. If Rosenfeld were still alive, I knew he would have found a way to send us a letter, a card. The Devil you know...

CHAPTER 28

THURSDAY, JUNE 18, 1942: *TROUBLEMAKERS*
were spreading word today about a forthcoming resettlement
action. We are becoming immune to such news.

On Saturday, June 15, I looked forward to walking with Regina to the park, but the rain came. It cleared by the afternoon, but it was too late. As I sat in the dust of the flat, I thought how the sudden change in weather was like the abrupt changes in our lives in the ghetto. Each break in the monotony and misery of our existence was heralded by rumors, clouds foretelling a storm, spreading darkness before each awful event.

The Chairman railed endlessly against the troublemakers who spread these forecasts as if they were the cause of all the problems threatening his smooth-running machine. He didn't grasp that the machine was not his anymore if it had ever been. Miriam didn't seem to understand that either. She blamed the Eldest of the Jews as if he were the one causing us to suffer. Our different views simmered like volcanic lava, building pressure until the inevitable explosions. I had to escape.

Work, tedious, repetitive, each day like the last, was calming. I secreted myself in our chamber, prioritized the mail, and dashed off entries, some of which I now signed. It was all routine, automatic. Except when Heilig or Cukier got some bee up their nose and got into a rare heated debate, as we had when we started this task. Singer and Rosenfeld had such passion in those early days. Their battles tried my patience, as I played mediator. Now I would have welcomed any break from the staleness of our task. We were just doing what was necessary to survive.

Few events aroused our shell-shocked emotions. On Sunday, June 14, the announcement that a campaign had been declared against men with beards reminded me of the day when Rosenfeld was attacked and forcibly shaved by a German soldier. We were incensed by this indignity to our gentle friend. Today, the announcement merited little discussion.

"Why does the Chairman bother with such trivial matters?" Heilig asked.

Cukier, ever the Chairman's defender, justified this hunt for bearded men as essential to the impression that everyone was working. "The Chairman has warned them time and time again to shave the bloody things off, but do they listen?"

I knew the Germans hated the beards as a symbol of Jewish orthodoxy. What the Germans ordered, the Chairman carried out before they seized the opportunity. He issued an order that anyone not clean shaven would lose their job. Even those who clung to their beards for religious reasons knew that could mean deportation. I thought of my friend, Dr. Rosenfeld, and how he had cowered in the corner that terrible day. It was the dawn of my awakening to what our occupiers could do to us at their whim. I missed him.

To break the monotony, and escape from our workroom, I volunteered to visit the hospital where a surprise German inspection had taken place.

The hospital director invited me into his office. "Biebow himself was here," he said, looking anxiously at the door.

"The German ghetto administrator?" I asked. "Why would he be interested in our hospital?"

"I think they want to shut it down."

"The Chairman would never allow that," I said. "What would happen to all the patients?"

The director held up his hands. "God only knows."

I assured him the hospital was under the Chairman's protection.

He asked a nurse to escort me around. The building was run-down, paint peeling and the smell of urine, overwhelming. The staff, exhausted, in soiled coats, appeared to be working hard to help the poor wretches housed within its overcrowded wards. The patients were in various states of mental illness. Confusion was evident in many faces, glazed eyes staring at the walls. Others rocked back and forth in chairs or on the floor. The worst were those strapped into beds, shriveled bodies, flesh barely covering their bones. I felt closed in with the misery all around me, terrible conditions caused by the Nazis. I couldn't wait to get away after viewing the first floor.

What would the Germans do with all these wretched souls if they shut the place down? I decided to talk to Neftalin. If anyone had answers, it would be the trusted Deputy to the Chairman.

There was a line of people outside his office, a Jewish guard maintaining order. I waited impatiently for my turn, mulling over what I would say. When he saw me, a smile appeared. "Engineer, it is good to see a friendly face." He looked tired, but his hair was still slicked back, and though his suit seemed a bit worn, he wore a tie and looked the part.

"Sir, do you have a minute for me?" I asked, standing before his desk as I had when I'd first been summoned by the Chairman.

"Please, sit? It has been a difficult morning."

"I hope I do not add to your troubles." I offered a friendly smile.

"That would be a change since I usually bring mine to you." He smiled back. "I would offer you cognac, but there is none."

"I don't drink anyway. Thank you."

"Now, what can I do for you?"

I thought of the things I could ask for Miriam and Regina but realized those were out of his control. I wasn't sure what powers he, or the Chairman, still had. "Sir—"

"Please, call me Henryk. I'm tired of always the impersonal greetings.

Now, please do not hesitate. Our trust in your loyalty has been well-justified. What can I do for you?"

"I've just returned from the hospital on Wesolo Street."

His face darkened. "I'm not sure how much help I can be."

"The director said Biebow, the German ghetto administrator, had been there."

"That is correct."

"He says the Germans want to shut it down." When Neftalin didn't answer, I asked, "Is the Chairman aware of this intention?"

"We are aware. The inspection was not announced, or the Chairman would have attended."

"Do they want to shut down the facility?"

Neftalin shifted in his chair and replied, "They sent an order to vacate the hospital. They want to use the building for a factory."

"It is true?"

Neftalin leaned forward. "You must understand, the Chairman objected strenuously to the authorities explaining the importance of the hospital. He has consistently resisted any action of the authorities that he deems would hurt our people. You, of all people, must know this. You've seen ample evidence."

I said nothing, waiting for him to continue.

Neftalin glanced at the door. "Despite all our Chairman's efforts, his earnest pleas, he received a written reply that there were plenty of small buildings available for a hospital, and, I'm quoting, "as for the sick, there was no possibility of saving their lives as things stood now." End quote."

"No possibility of saving their lives?"

"That is a direct quote."

I was shocked by Biebow's icy death sentence. "All?" I asked.

Neftalin stood. "Believe me, my friend, the Chairman, as always, is making every effort to avert the elimination of the hospital. The danger of that happening is, however, quite real."

My mind raced. Miriam was right. We'd been fooling ourselves.

Biebow said it best: "No possibility of saving their lives." The Germans had the power of life and death. One command from them and every patient in the hospital was 'punctuated.' An order from Berlin and the ghetto was gone. Kaput.

Neftalin said, "I'm sorry. I have work to do, Engineer."

I saw a resignation in him I'd never seen before. I rose and turned away silently, not even thanking him. All I could think about were those sad-looking patients. What would the Nazis do with them?

I was at the door when Neftalin said, "We must all pray now for our Chairman."

We must all pray for ourselves, I thought, as the door slowly closed.

CHAPTER 29

SATURDAY, JUNE 20, 1942: THE CARPENTERS WORK-SHOP
Has received an order to construct a gallows for 10 people. The structure was built and was picked up today.

It was like holding a hot coal in my hand. "Heilig, you wrote this. Is that all there is?"

"My informant in the workshop said the German authorities ordered it."

"I knew the Chairman would never order such a monstrosity," Cukier said, "The Germans want to frighten us with it."

"It is frightening," I said, noting the tension in the Weasel's demeanor. "The question is, will they use it?"

"The Chairman will never allow that," Cukier said. "Look how he fought for the hospital. You reported it as if it was a done deal, but see, because of his protests, nothing has happened. You need to have more confidence in our leadership."

"I hope you are right. A gallows for one victim was frightening enough. Remember the public hanging?"

"That was ages ago. There has been no repetition. No, this is strictly for show."

Heilig, who had been silent, blurted out, "They have hung Jews in other towns. Nobody knows how many."

"Well, it won't be allowed here," Cukier said. "Let them build their monstrous gallows. Let them put it up as a monument to their cruelty.

The chairman will never let them use it."

Cukier's coughs ended the discussion.

I said, "There's another meat shortage. It looks like we're back on meals of bread and ersatz coffee."

Heilig piped up. "The management of the Meat Clearinghouse states they have just received a small shipment of horse meat that will be disinfected—a one-day delay—and then distributed to the four remaining public kitchens."

Miriam had served me a piece of sausage a few days earlier. It immediately made my stomach churn. I'd gone to work experiencing gut pain for several days. I thanked God that with our meager rations, the bit of sausage had been small. God knows what it might have done to me if it had been larger.

Heilig held up an official proclamation. "This one was issued on June 19, by the Eldest of the Jews. It is addressed to all departments, enterprises, and workshops."

"Not another one?" I said, tired of all the proclamations and circulars.

"You'll love this one. "By order of the authorities, I am informing you that residents of the ghetto are obliged to greet all German officials, whether they are in civilian clothing or in uniform.'"

"What?" I couldn't believe the Chairman thought this was worthy of using our scant supply of paper, another shortage among the many that plagued us.

Heilig held up his hand. "May I continue? "When workshops or offices are inspected, or during visits from members of the Ghetto Administration, everyone must rise upon hearing the command 'Attention!'. The suspension of work during an inspection will continue until the moment when the command 'Back to work' is heard. Workshop directors should appoint persons to deliver these two commands during an inspection or visit so that these greetings may proceed smoothly. I recommend that trial runs be made after receipt of this circular." Thus saith the Chairman."

"May I see that?" Cukier held out his hand.

Heilig handed it to him.

Cukier read it, then crumpled and threw it on the floor.

Heilig retrieved the crumpled paper. "It's official. I'm including it."

"Fine," Cukier said. "Nobody will read this shit anyway."

"So, who will you choose?" I asked, aiming playful eyes at our leader.

"For what?"

"As our official greeter," I replied. "We need to run practice drills. The Chairman has ordered them."

"For heaven's sake," Cukier exploded. "Okay. Fine. You may have the honor of greeting the Germans when they arrive. Do you think you are capable of handling such a responsible duty?" He turned away in disgust. "People are eating shit, dying in the streets, being shipped out to God knows where, and he wants practice drills for saluting our damn oppressors?"

"Julian, what is wrong?" I was surprised by such an outburst from our usually calm friend.

He threw up his hands. "What's wrong? What the hell is wrong? Everything! Everything is wrong. Everything we've experienced since the Nazis invaded, everything they have done to us, to our families, our friends." He choked up. "They starve us, want to hang us, ship us here and there at their whim. What is wrong? Engineer, my last friend on this planet, even you, the proponent of logic, know everything is wrong."

Heilig looked stunned.

I wrapped my arms around Julian and held him close to me. His breathing and trembling reminded me of Miriam. He was almost as thin and fragile. "You are ill, my friend. You need a vacation. You should go to the hospital—"

He pulled away from me. "Hospital? Vacation? What is wrong with you? Don't you see that all that is saving me from the clutches of these monsters are the wings of the Chairman, and only if I work. I can't rest. I can't stay at home. There is no medicine. There are few doctors.

Even the hospital is threatened now!"

I had to calm him, afraid he would have an apoplectic fit. And if he didn't, Heilig, who had backed into a corner, might. "Julian, you said yourself, we are safe here. If anyone is safe, it is the upper echelon of the ghetto administration. The Chairman needs us, and the Germans need him to keep their army supplied."

Julian raised his shirt. Emblazoned on his chest was the Latin letter B.

CHAPTER 30

WEDNESDAY, JUNE 24, 1942: A SHOOTING
At around midnight on June 19, a young man was shot to death on the other side of the barbed wire...

How do you offer hope to a condemned man? Even days after Julian had shown us the secret he had harbored for so many months, the letter painted on his chest, I was unable to deal with it. The knowledge that at any time this man I had come to love might be plucked away and lost to me forever was unbearable. I knew he was sick. Most people were. This was different. My friend was living with a sword dangling over his head. Would he be the next Rosenfeld? I wished Singer would appear, but knew Cukier, stubborn, refusing to yield to the disease, would never allow our errant friend to risk his life to save him. And where was Singer? All his promises to save Miriam and Regina had come to nothing.

"Here we go again!" Heilig sounded as if he was about to launch into a joke. "There was another shooting."

"Not another?" Cukier remarked. "Another man? By the barbed wire?"

"Do they know who it was?" I asked, always fearing the worst.

Heilig said, "Only that he was young. Hey, he was on the other side of the barbed wire." He looked at me. "I wonder if he was trying to get out or in."

Cukier interrupted. "Who cares? He's one of the countless idiots who try. Engineer, run down to Lagiewnicka Street, at the corner of

Balut Market. There is a new museum being established." He shrugged his shoulders. "I know the Chairman is looking for ways to employ people, but a museum?"

"That is strange." I grabbed my coat and checking that he was alright, I headed to the front of the building. It was no longer unusual to see armed German guards in our halls. They were an ominous presence. I missed the Jewish police.

The streets were deserted. The Chairman had ordered that nobody was to be seen as idle, not even children. I held my I.D. as I made my way to the far end of Balut Market, to the corner of Lagiewnicka Street. I recognized the building as the former premises of the defunct Department of Vegetables. The Chairman loved creating departments for almost everything, but a museum? I would have laughed, but all these departments at least gave the impression that all was under control. It was lunacy, but it was something to stem the tide that was drowning Jews in other ghettos.

I entered the building and was surprised to see a flurry of activity. I asked who was in charge and was brought to a man in rabbinical attire. He introduced himself as Rabbi Hirszberg, Emanuel. He seemed aloof, a bit snooty, but also more fit than most of the people of the ghetto. After droning on about the uniqueness of his museum, he guided me around the building. I was surprised by the artistry of the displays, most featuring large dolls whose hands and heads were made of porcelain. I could not help commenting about the beauty of the garments. "We don't seem many of these here anymore," I said, noting the faces lacked features.

The rabbi replied, "We have many fine artists, sculptors, painters, and tailors working on this." He showed me the beginnings of a lavish wedding display.

I thought he looked distracted. Was the task overwhelming?

The Rabbi stood by a young woman leaning over a drawing pad. "My daughter and I have been working in the city up to now... by order of the authorities." He gave me a sharp look, and the daughter looked up, a nervous expression on her face. He signaled me to follow him.

He led me to a back room, more a spacious closet, where there were a large number of drawings on a table and dolls in various stages of completion. He looked furtively out the door and then said, "This work is being done as a function of the Research Department, to produce exhibits of Jewish life in the ghetto. My daughter and I are experts in this field."

"I didn't know the Chairman had a Research Department," I said.

The Rabbi shook his head. "We are operating by direct order of the German authorities." He looked uneasily at the open door.

"You are not authorized by the Chairman?"

He signaled me to lower my voice, checking around the door again. "No. The Research Department was created by the authorities to establish museums here and in other cities."

"Are you saying the Germans by-passed the Chairman? I don't understand. Why would the Nazis want a museum that celebrates a culture they hate, a people they want to destroy?"

The professor slid several sketches toward me. He peered anxiously out the door again. "These are some of the designs." He arranged the drawings flat on the table.

I leaned close and realized instantly that far from glorifying our ancient culture and rites, the displays were cruel, satirical depictions of the people they wanted the world to hate. I pulled away from the drawings and stared into the professor's face. I saw a ghost-like image of fear in his pupils.

"You understand now?" He grabbed up the sketches and resumed his official posture.

"Thank you for your time," I said, aware that a German policeman was outside the door observing us.

"Please visit again once we are open," he said.

The policeman, looking bored, stepped just far enough away for me to pass.

I hurried from the museum as if rushing from the scene of a brutal murder. The Germans had by-passed our Chairman and were installing in our central square a monument to their bigotry. Not satisfied any longer with two-dimensional caricatures of Jews with long hook noses, unkept stringy hair, black filthy-looking clothes, with matching black hats, they were erecting life-sized dolls and displays, to permanently showcase their twisted view of Jewish culture. Oh God, I thought, is there no limit to what these oppressors will subject us to?

I hurried back to our room, but it was empty. A chill ran down my spine. I know it was wrong to assume the worst, but it was realistic. People were disappearing all around us. No warning. No warrant. One second here, and the next gone. I collapsed in my chair. Even with shortages of paper, ink, pencils, and pens, the stream of notes kept flowing. I thought of the unnamed young man who had been shot. I flicked through Heilig's listing of the newly departed. Was it Singer?

I breathed a sigh of relief. The boy was 24 and named Rafal Kutner. Alone in the room, I let my head fall onto my crossed arms, the memory of those hellish dolls burning into my brain.

CHAPTER 31

SUNDAY, JUNE 28, 1942
   On Thursday, the 25th of this month, a session of the Rabbinate was suddenly called, and a letter sent by the Chairman read. Because of large orders, the woodworking workshop must be increased, and the old cemetery that abuts the grounds of the workshop is to be used as a lumberyard.

"What happens to the headstones?" I asked.

Heilig replied. "The Germans want them as paving." He spat on the floor.

Cukier was a zombie, no reaction, staring at blood stains on his handkerchief.

I said, "The Chairman won't allow that."

Heilig shook his head. "The Rabbinate Council appealed for his intercession, but concluded with, "please save whatever can be saved?"

"Please save whatever can be saved?" I repeated it, wishing I had the power to save Miriam and Regina, but feeling as helpless as the rabbis.

"The hospital for the mentally ill is being threatened too," Heilig said.

"The one on Wesolo Street?" I had visited the site earlier.

He nodded.

"Maybe they'll have their way this time if even our dead are not safe."

Cukier still didn't respond.

"Another shooting by the barbed wire," Heilig smiled. "Don't worry, it was a woman this time."

How could I feel relieved when a woman had been shot? But I did.

Heilig slammed the paper on the table. "This Eva Landau was by the barbed wire and asked the sentry to shoot her. She is judged to have dared him because she attempted to make her way through the wire right before his eyes. So, he shot her. End of discussion."

I remembered the sight of another woman bleeding to death as she hung on the barbs of that goddamn fence. I'd almost died thinking it was Miriam. As depressed as she sometimes seemed, so long as Regina was with her I wasn't afraid of her trying something so desperate.

Cukier suddenly stood. "Heil Hitler!" He shouted and shot his arm into the air. Then, as we recoiled in shock, he burst into insane laughter.

Alarmed, I raced to his side.

"I'm fine," he said, shoving me away. "The whole damn world is insane, but I'm fine." He shoved an official circular from the Chairman into my hand. "Go ahead. Read it aloud." He walked to the window and pulled the shade. He stared out of the boarded window as if enjoying a view of the sea, a smile appearing on his gaunt face. "The whole world is insane, and I'm leading the pack."

I glanced at Heilig and read the circular. "Proclamation No. 387 concerning the obligation to greet all German officials, both in uniform and in civilian clothing. This proclamation directs the populace's attention to the fact that the obligation is not being observed scrupulously."

"You've got to be kidding?" I cast a glance at Cukier who was still staring out the boarded window as if at a water view of the ocean. "Clerks driving past in automobiles should also be greeted. Order Service men and firemen are obliged to express their respects—"

"Respects?" Heilig asked. "For Nazis?"

"That is what he says, 'to express their respects by coming to attention.'

"In the middle of a fire?"

"Here's the rest, "The civilian population is obliged to remove any head covering. Women and persons not wearing hats are to perform the greeting by inclining their heads forward." Oh shit! Listen to the last sentence!"

"I can hardly wait," Heilig said.

I had to look to be sure he wasn't Singer. "Those failing to observe this obligation are under threat of severe punishment." I dropped the circular on my pile. "Off with their head," I cried, parodying Lewis Carroll's mad queen. "If you don't bow your head, you lose it."

Cukier turned around. "You're right. It is Alice in Wonderland, but there is no end in sight for all this insanity." He straightened up. "We must persist. Whatever they throw at us, we must persist." He settled back in his chair.

I returned to my post. I began to write a summary of events for the month of June: "It had begun so optimistically. We were promised increased food rations, but that hadn't materialized, and hunger was worse than before. The number of deaths, even with much less population shot up from 40 per day to between 70 and 80. Everywhere, the hungry and feeble were stumbling along the streets, unable to work, unable to even get to work. And still the orders from the Germans for our goods kept coming in. The Chairman, true to his word, was valiantly struggling to employ everyone, even children 8-10 years old. But productivity was falling. We were just not strong enough. Laborers were completely exhausted. We were all in a no-exit situation. Deportation loomed as the punishment if we succumbed to weakness, rampant diseases, and the debilitating pain of hunger." I read my words and shivered, especially at the final sentence: "The ghetto has not only become a labor camp where there is no place for people who are not working, but also some sort of Nietzschean experimental laboratory from which only the 'very strong' emerge in one piece..." I expected Cukier to ax my entry, or at least question it. I no longer cared.

He read it twice. Without comment, he placed it on the pile of all the other pages of our chronicle.

I should have felt proud of his acceptance of my entry, but there was no time. More work lay before me. As I gleaned through the notes, I glanced at Cukier. He was not strong enough to be among the few who might survive this "experiment" of the Aryan race. Could Miriam and I survive it? How many Jews had already become victim to Hitler's inhuman testing? How many "undesirables"?

I understood at last that numbers barely scratched the surface of all the horror stories hate had created. "We are not numbers!" I wanted to scream to the uncaring world, to our deaf and blind God, but in Hitler's world view, that was what we were.

CHAPTER 32

M ONDAY, JULY 6, 1942
The number of ghetto residents— 102,500—is the lowest since the ghetto came into existence.
Eighty-six people died in the ghetto today. (The death rate continues its alarming increase.)

Cukier was showing up late for work, but miraculously he was showing up. Coughing and sputtering had become far worse, as had his temper. "The food situation," he rasped hoarsely, "is totally disgraceful! I wouldn't feed a pig this rancid shit!"

I had to agree with him. Recent shipments of meat had arrived that were green, yellow, or white, supposed to be made into sausage. The Meat Clearinghouse contacted the authorities and complained that the rotten meat would sicken our workers, so two officials were sent to check it out and ultimately decided to hold it until veterinary doctors could determine if it could still be used. More and more of our food was not fit for human consumption, but it was all we were given. Rancid butter and spoiled flour, all unusable elsewhere, were good enough for us. We had a choice of risking disease or starving. The zombies were on the street again, risking arrest, tempting German guns, but the Chairman had more important concerns.

It was Neftalin who brought us the news.

I was dealing with another troubling rumor: the four kitchens still operating were replacing meals with only soup again. The Department of Soup Kitchens, one of our infinite number of departments, claimed they knew nothing of this, so I was writing it up for our Chronicle, mostly because there seemed lately, perhaps a reflection of our decreasing population, to be a dearth of news. When I saw Neftalin staring at me, I knew something was wrong.

"Where is Julian?" He asked.

"He'll be here soon," I replied. "He usually stops to see you first."

Heilig was watching me with his weasel eyes. He claimed he had not heard from Singer, but could I trust him? Could I trust any of them?

The door inched open.

Cukier, leaning on a cane, top missing, stepped into the room. "Why are you here?" His voice was a low croak. He leaned against the wall.

Neftalin brushed back his hair which had grown long and stringy. "I have two items for you. First, the Chairman posted a new Proclamation, No. 388."

I waited for Heilig to remark, as he usually did, "What, another one?" but he remained silent.

Neftalin continued, "It is a notice that the Eldest of the Jews should be informed about any places in the city (outside the ghetto) where merchandise or objects of value are being kept or hidden."

"This is old news. The Chairman has demanded this numerous times."

Neftalin nodded. "The Chairman adds that houses are being demolished in certain districts of the city of Lodz. Anyone who reveals where merchandise is hidden will receive cash based on an appraisal by the Department, with a percentage deducted for the Community, of course."

Of course, I thought, wondering whose coffers were being enriched by this new decree.

Neftalin continued, "No one should fear punitive sanctions if they turn these things in now."

"Do you think most people will believe that?" Heilig asked.

"Our beloved Chairman assures no punishment." Neftalin scowled at Heilig.

"He does, but what about the Germans?"

"The Chairman promises no punishment," Neftalin repeated.

Heilig gave me a meaningful look. "It doesn't matter. I have nothing to hide. The Germans have it all."

"My situation too," I said.

"Item 2?" Cukier asked, looking as if the whole thing was boring him.

Neftalin aimed his eyes at me. "I want you to record that the chairman is making great progress—"

"We always do report this," Cukier interrupted.

Neftalin sighed. "Please, allow me to finish? This is important." He pulled out a note he had written. "It is essential you report 'verbatim' that the Chairman has made every possible effort to employ children over the age of ten."

"What's this?" An alarm bell rang in my head.

Neftalin's eyes shot toward me. "Especially those who have been previously stamped by the medical commissions."

I interrupted. "My God! My God! The rumors are true?"

Neftalin turned to me. "What rumors specifically? There are so many flying around."

"About the imminent deportation of children." I choked saying it.

Heilig added, "I've heard such rumors too. You must answer. Panic is everywhere."

Neftalin stood, his eyes angry. "These are all unfounded. You can say, 'This is categorically denied by authoritative circles.' Do not use my name."

I was terrified. "I have a daughter, one-year-old. You know this. Tell me the truth, should I be afraid?"

Neftalin's face softened. "No. The chairman loves our children, all children. He will protect your child with all his might and authority. You should know this." He walked to the door. "The Chairman, our beloved Eldest of the Jews, counts on you to record his earnest efforts to protect our most precious treasure, our children. Someday, people will want to know…" He looked upset as he left the room.

That night, unable to shake my fear, I finally told Miriam the truth. "Miriam, I was sworn to secrecy to obtain this position, but you need to know now. My job in the Archives makes me privy to the inner workings of the Eldest of the Jews. I am sometimes, not always, able to learn what is happening, sometimes even before the yentas."

Miriam stared at me. "I suspected as much."

"I couldn't tell you. It has been a terrible obligation…keeping this from you. I'm truly sorry."

"Thank you for finally sharing the truth with me. But why now?" She eyed me with suspicion.

I hated telling her but had no choice. "My superior, Deputy Neftalin, came into our room today. He made me aware that…well, certain rumors are flying…which you may have heard…which may be frightening to you."

"There are always frightening rumors," Miriam said, her voice cold. "What rumors forced you to tell the truth at last?"

I had to bite the bullet. "Henryk denies there is any truth to them. He…It's about the possible…it will never happen…the Chairman will never allow the deportation of children from our ghetto."

Miriam's hands were clenched tight in her lap. Her eyes darted to Regina in her crib. "Tell me the damn truth at last? Should I be afraid?"

"The Deputy says no. He swore it up and down."

"But you don't believe him?"

"I'm not certain."

"You don't believe your damn Chairman?"

The tension in her voice told me she was holding back, could become explosive at any wrong word. "I believe the Eldest of the Jews is doing everything possible to protect our children. He loves them. He's shown that time and time again. I believe he would never allow anything to hurt them."

"I believe he loves children. Yes, that much I do believe," Miriam said. "So, what is behind your sudden honesty?"

In other circumstances, her petulance would have infuriated me, but this wasn't the time. "I don't know if the Chairman can protect them?" I quickly added, "I know with all my heart he wants to, but can he? Can anyone?"

Miriam's eyes were daggers. "I told you we should leave here. I begged you. I begged you over and over—"

"I know. I tried. I tried. Believe me, I've been trying."

She looked surprised.

I looked imploringly into her eyes and swallowed my pride. "Months ago, I asked Singer—"

"You asked him? You really did?"

"Yes."

"You've seen him?"

"You haven't?" Now, I was surprised. I assumed Singer had been secretly meeting with her for weeks.

"No! Of course not! I've been worried sick about him. Why didn't you tell me you've seen him?" A look at my face and she knew. "You are a foolish man. I would never violate my vows."

"Not even if you love him?" I bit my lip. It was the most painful thing I ever had to say to her. "I would understand."

Miriam stood over me. "No. I would never betray you...not even if I loved him."

I didn't ask if she loved him. I couldn't bear it if she confirmed my suspicions. Did I believe her? It didn't matter. I fought tears in my eyes.

Miriam's eyes were aimed at me. "You should have told me. You should have trusted me."

"Yes."

"Yes."

"I'm sorry."

Miriam shook her head sadly. "What did Oscar say? Can he help us get out of here?"

"He said he would try."

"That's good. He's very capable."

And I'm not, I thought, regretting I didn't accept his invitations to use the black market, to form connections, that might have helped us. "Yes, if anyone can help, I also thought it was Singer."

"You thought?"

"You haven't seen or heard from him?"

"I already told you, no."

"I haven't either."

"You're not lying again?"

"No. I'll never lie to you again. I was wrong to do that...to not trust you." I felt miserable. "It was him. I didn't trust Oscar. Maybe he knew that? Maybe that's why he never contacted me again." An idea came to me. "Maybe if you try and contact him? He loves you. He told me...he loves you."

"He told you that?"

I hesitated. Pulling myself up from the chair, I went to my briefcase and pulled out the crumpled letter. I flattened it and handed it to her.

"You've had this all along?" She stared at me.

"Yes. I had it, but I was shocked...I had no inkling. Please, imagine how I felt."

She began reading.

"I should have given it to you. How could I? I was afraid you would take Regina and leave me."

She finished the letter silently and then returned it. "It is addressed to all of us. You are a fool." She rose from the chair and walked to the crib. "You cost us a friend who might have saved our child." She reached down and pulled the thin coverlet over Regina. "I would never have done anything to risk her...or hurt you."

"I'll find him," I said, hoping I sounded more confident than I felt. "I'll get him to help you and Regina escape from here."

Miriam didn't reply. She removed her dress and stood before me in her chemise.

I waited for her to beckon me to come to bed. I would have done anything to make up to her for not sharing Singer's letter, his love for her…for us. I wanted so desperately to just hold her, hold her against me.

No signal came. I watched silently as Miriam lowered herself onto the bed and pulled the worn coverlet up to her face. I trembled, overwhelmed with guilt when I heard her sobbing into her pillow.

CHAPTER 33

SATURDAY, JULY 11, 1942

The morning after I finally shared Singer's letter with Miriam, I cornered Heilig before Cukier arrived. I pinned him against the wall, begged, threatened, begged again, but he kept repeating that he had not seen Singer and knew nobody who had. I asked him if he knew of anyone else who had dealings with the secret market but didn't reveal why. I was so desperate to find Singer, to get any help. The Weasel may have guessed my motive, but never let on.

Day after day, I cajoled, begged, and threatened poor Heilig. What a joke. Me, the Engineer, forced to resort to threats of physical violence. I was surprised he didn't burst out laughing, but he looked frightened. He swore up-and-down that he would help if he could. I believed him. There had to be something else I could do.

I began to take every opportunity to leave the safety of our room, search the streets, praying I might find someone who knew Singer, or of someone else who might help me get Regina and Miriam away. I had decided, was resigned, to remain in the ghetto, if that's what it would take to save them.

Cukier was reading a report about deportees shipped here from Kalisz, a town in Poznan that had contained over 20,000 Jews, comprising 35 percent of the general population. "Damn the Germans! They emptied another ghetto." He looked exhausted. "We should get the details of this."

"I'll go," Heilig said, rising from his chair.

I pushed him back down. "No. I'll go. You stay here and finish today's work."

Heilig knew better than to argue. He settled back in his chair.

I was gone before Julian could protest. The hallway was swarming with Gestapo and Nazi officials. I was glad to escape the building. I headed toward the Central Station, showing my identification where Order Service police were stationed. Germans were guarding the depot. I couldn't get close to the train.

Cukier had reported that 500 people had been sent here from Kalisz and were housed in the old barracks. I decided to try my luck there. I hesitated. Order Service men surrounded the building. I summoned my courage. My pass got me through.

There was an acrid smell. It reminded me of a wet furry dog, thick and musty. Blankets were spread across the floor. Many of the people looked stunned. A few were moaning or talking to themselves. The Jewish police were watching them from various points in the open expanse. I breathed a sigh of relief when I saw a few children lying or sitting on the blankets. I had feared the worst, that they had been separated from their parents and sent to wherever the Nazis sent children, the elderly and the infirm. By now, everyone in the ghetto suspected the worst. All the used clothing and shoes shipped into our warehouses, being sorted by women like Miriam, made us all suspect what we still found impossible to believe. The idea that Germans could kill so many Jews in such mass numbers defied logic. That any humans could have such an absence of morality, be so without conscience, could hate so much, and manage something so atrocious, was incomprehensible. But how could we explain the evidence mounting up in our storage buildings?

I approached a fairly-well-dressed man about my age. "Are you okay?" I asked.

He looked up at me with dull eyes. "We are from Kalisz."

"I know."

"Where are we?"

"You're in the Lodz...Litzmannstadt ghetto. You're safe here."

He looked doubtful.

"Our Eldest of the Jews, Chairman Rumkowski, has turned us into an industrial center. The Germans depend on us—"

The man burst into bitter laughter.

It frightened me, but I had to know the truth. "Can you tell me what happened to your ghetto?"

He puckered his lips. "You said this is the Lodz ghetto? Our Chairman, Gustaf Hahn was here in January."

"I remember him."

"We had rumors that the entire ghetto was to be cleansed of Jews. Of course, we didn't believe…so many rumors. We were like you, most employed in factories. We thought that would protect us. Nothing protects from the Germans. Nothing."

"We're making things for their military."

"I see. That's why they sent the last of us here. I see." He straightened a crease on the blanket. "We are the last shoemakers, tailors, electricians, locksmiths, sandal-makers—craftsmen and machine workers. The rest? All were deported to places unknown." He looked plaintively at me. "Do you know where they are? Sir, do you know?"

"No. We've had letters from some rural areas, but a few only."

"I see. We all lived in fear for months. A German manufacturer set up a workshop for mending army uniforms. We thought that would protect us. It did…for a while. The order to vacate Kalisz came without a moment's notice."

"You had no warning at all?"

"No. It happened on Monday, the 6th this month. The Gestapo came to all our workplaces informing the Jews to prepare to leave the ghetto within an hour."

"One hour?"

"We rushed back to our homes and packed a few belongings in feverish haste. You can imagine how much we left behind. Although, in truth, there was little the Germans had not confiscated."

"What happened next?" Did I really want to hear?

"We were all herded to the train station. The screaming and curses still echo in my head." He held his ears with his hands. "We were there the entire night. It was terrible, but then they separated us into two groups." He trembled. "Only those appearing to the Germans as skilled workers were included in our transport."

"But you have some children with you?" I was desperate to salvage some morsel of hope.

He gazed around the room. "Children?" Tears came to his eyes. "Yes, children. We were able to smuggle only a few with us. The majority were taken. They said they would return them. Have they arrived?" He looked hopefully at me.

"I'm sorry."

He closed his eyes. "I won't tell the few mothers we have with us. There are only 500 of us here. Nearly 20,000 scattered all over." He let out a deep sigh. "I hope this war ends soon so we can be with our friends and families again."

I didn't have the heart to tell him what I now believed about the fate of deportees. "I share your hope, my friend. How did you manage to hide the children?"

"The Germans only sent four rail cars for 500 people. They said we could not take our baggage with us, except small hand-held bundles. They promised the baggage would rejoin us here. Has it?"

I shook my head. "Sir, the children?"

He nodded. "We had five hundred people crammed into four cars. A few children could be smuggled in. Our women and children haven't arrived yet?"

"No. Not yet." I was about to leave when the man said, "Your Chairman said he will check on our missing baggage?"

"The Chairman was here?"

"Yes. He spoke to several of us. He was eager to know everything about what happened to the Jews of Kalisz. He said he would try to get our baggage returned or give us clothing and bedding. He said he has warehouses with ample stock."

That he does, I thought, recalling Miriam's description of the mountains of used clothing.

"He also promised us jobs, and said that everyone who works hard, who does not shirk, will be protected." He looked at me again with hopeful eyes. "We all feared deportation. It hung over us…and yet, here we are, safe at last. In Lodz, you said?"

I smiled, hoping to comfort him. "Yes, you are safe here…in Lodz."

"Lodz. A great city."

"God be with you, my friend." I left him sitting on his coverlet and was about to flee the building when I spotted another man sitting on a blanket isolated from the others. He was wearing shabbier clothing and was crying. I approached him cautiously, fearing he might be insane. "Sir, are you alright?" He didn't seem to hear me, so I repeated, "Sir, are you alright?"

He looked up.

I thought I saw deathly fear in his eyes. I wanted to leave, but something in his face held me in check. "Are you from Kalisz," I asked

He shook his head.

"Where are you from, my friend?"

"Zdunska Wola," he said, still crying and now rocking back and forth like some brain-damaged child.

"That's near here." I was surprised he was from our province. I recalled that it was a small town, perhaps 10,000 Jews. I recalled that Jews accounted for about 40 percent of the entire population of the town. "You have nothing to be afraid of," I said, trying to calm him. "You're in the Lodz ghetto. You're safe now."

His eyes shot up at me. "They're gone…gone. Only a few left…"

"All 10,000?" I asked, finding this shocking. "They weren't sent here with you?"

"They're gone." He rocked back and forth again, and then his eyes met mine, and he said, "Shot…murdered…men, women…children."

I reeled back from him. Was it true? Looking at him, a grown man, shivering in terror, I knew it was. I felt panicky, terrified, not wanting to believe. I raced from the building, not stopping until back in the Balut Market. So many buildings, once packed like sardine cans, were now empty. Where were the people? I stared at the gray warehouses of clothing, backpacks, bedding. It was more than I could bear. "Goddamn! Where is Singer?"

Still shaking, my mind cracking, I returned to our room, the only sanctuary for me in the whole goddamn ghetto. I had to gather my thoughts. Was I insane? Was it a horrific nightmare? I focused my brain on writing the entry. No one might ever read it, but if the Chairman did, he would see what I saw: how Kalisz, and too many other 'safe' ghettos, had been brutally liquidated. Maybe he would hear the bullets smashing into the skulls of men, women, and children…oh God, children…bullets I heard echoing in my brain hours, days, after hearing that distraught man, barely comprehending what he'd witnessed, what he was saying, in that cavern of broken souls. Maybe, at long last, our Chairman would wake up and realize that working for the Nazis would not save us. It was time to find something that would. Singer had been right all along. It was time to fight the wolves.

CHAPTER 34

T**UESDAY, JULY 21, 1942:** 13,000 Children

    I jumped to attention when Heilig read the title of the entry he was writing.

"Thirteen thousand children had by the 20th of this month been employed by the School Department in various Community workshops as apprentices," he continued. "That is good news for a change."

Oh, thank God, I thought, fearing a much different narrative. With all the rumors swirling around about children being deported...but Neftalin had said that no matter what happened in other ghettos, it would never be allowed here. We had leverage thanks to the forward thinking of our great chairman, Rumkowski.

"Are you alright?" Heilig asked. "You turned pale as a ghost."

"Yes. Fine. Please finish?" It's strange how I couldn't warm up to him. He had never done anything to earn my enmity. It was just that he wasn't Singer. I should have hated that bastard, but I couldn't. I envied him. He was everything I was not, including being a puzzle, a mystery. Of course, that made him attractive to young women, especially young women with boring husbands.

"Engineer, are you here today?" Heilig asked.

"Yes! Dammit! Read! And stop worrying about me!" He just irritated the shit out of me. "Sorry. I was daydreaming. Please read?"

Heilig looked confused but continued reading his entry: "The department's success is proven by its finding employment for 1,800 young people between the ages of 10 and 17 in the first 20 days of

July." He looked at me. "That is a record for the ghetto."

"What is?" Cukier asked.

"The School Department found jobs for a record number of children, ages 10 to 17," I said before Heilig reread his entire entry with his blasted photographic whatever.

Cukier gave Heilig a weak smile. "I'm glad there is some good news. I just came from the Deputy's office. He handed me this memo. The authorities are liquidating the hospital at Wesolo Street."

"They're finally doing that?" I remembered my visit. "I was hoping they'd forgotten that one."

"That's where they treat people with tuberculosis," Cukier said.

Heilig added, "That disease is our worst enemy, the cause of many deaths here."

"I'd estimate three-quarters of the deaths in the ghetto," I said. "For once, I agree with Heilig, it is decimating the ghetto's population at a rate faster than anything else we are facing, including the war."

Cukier coughed, covered his mouth, and handed Heilig the memo. "Finish it."

Heilig read, "The hospital had 400 beds permanently assigned for Tuberculosis patients and a psychiatric ward that served 50. The conversion into a hospital with exemplary modern facilities in record time was the Eldest of the Jews' first monumental achievement. It was a great source of pride for him…and now, it will be gone."

Cukier coughed again. "At least he stopped them from putting its replacement in the cemetery."

"In the cemetery?" Heilig and I exclaimed.

Cukier laughed bitterly. "They were going to construct a hospital on the cemetery grounds, but thankfully, the Chairman succeeded in getting that order annulled."

I checked my notes. "Is that the hospital for which the Germans were going to charge us hundreds and thousands of marks?"

"Of course," Heilig said. "They force us to lose our hospital and then force us to pay them a fortune to build us a new one. It makes perfect sense. It's good business."

"I'm glad you approve. But the liquidation of the hospital for this highly contagious disease is disastrous," Cukier said.

What will they do with the patients? I thought, again fearing the worst.

Cukier pulled another sheet from his portfolio. "The Deputy tells me the recent arrivals, all without baggage, have been provided clothing, shoes, and undergarments by the Department of Resettled Persons, as ordered by the Eldest of the Jews."

Heiling looked up. "That must be a lot of clothing."

Cukier scanned the memo. "75,000 pieces of underwear alone."

"Where would we get so much clothing from?" Heilig asked.

Cukier glanced at me.

I assumed everyone knew. "Heilig, you do know about the trucks that have been arriving in the ghetto?"

"Who doesn't? There are many rumors about what is in them."

"They are not rumors. We've known for some time that the trucks are delivering various items of clothing to large storehouses designated by the authorities." I handed him the latest figures I'd received.

Heilig examined the document. A puzzled look appeared on his face. "What's this? Used shoes? Used?"

"You really didn't know?" I almost felt sorry for him.

He waved the paper at me. "How long have you known about this? Is this why you've been looking for—"

I cut him off. "Don't you have any friends? Hasn't anyone filled you in on what the hell is going on here?"

Heilig pushed his chair away and stood glaring at me. "I thought it was all rumors! You both knew? You didn't tell me?"

"I assumed you knew," I said. "Everyone seemed to know…or at least, suspect."

"We still don't know shit. We have no real confirmation of where these items come from," Cukier said. "The truth is, and you know it well, that we are almost totally isolated from the rest of Poland—"

"What about the newcomers? They must know something?" Heilig hissed.

Cukier sighed. "They know nothing more than we do. Yes, we suspect that some of our deportees may have met sad fates, but nobody can account for such large amounts of used clothing and shoes. The numbers are staggering, as our numbers man will attest."

I saw how upset Heilig was and tried to place a hand gently on his shoulder. He brushed it away. "Listen," I said. "I know what you're thinking. I've been thinking of it too, but for the life of me„ I cannot conceive how such an atrocity could be accomplished by the Germans. The sheer scope of this is incomprehensible. The logistics of such mass... executions... defies human capacity. It is implausible based on historical events to believe the Germans, any people, could find a method to exterminate—that is what such a mass execution would be called—Jews in such magnitude." Who was I convincing? Him or me?

"And yet, here are inexplicable tons and tons of used clothing," Heilig said. "You knew and should have told me that's why you wanted to see Singer again."

Damn him! I'd kept this from Julian.

"Again? You saw Singer?" Cukier shot at me, disbelief on his face.

I fired a curse at Heilig. "Yes. Months ago."

"You never said a damn word?"

Damn Weasel. "I saw him twice. He forced me to swear I would not reveal anything about him."

Cukier turned to Heilig, who I think realized he'd made a colossal mistake. "You know Singer? Tell me the truth?" He coughed into his rag.

Heilig looked like a trapped weasel. "He's my cousin."

"Your cousin?" I felt like pounding him in the face. I fell back in my chair.

Cukier smiled sadly. "Apparently, we all have secrets. The Nazis have succeeded in making Jews not trust Jews." He rose from his chair.

"If you see your cousin, please tell him I miss him. He was always honest." He looked at me and left the room.

"You sonofabitch," I hissed at Heilig. "Your cousin?"

The Weasel looked frightened. "What about you? You knew about the used clothing and never let on. Did you at least tell Oscar?" He slapped his forehead. "Idiot! I'm an idiot! That's why you wanted to get Miriam and your daughter away from here! Does Oscar know?"

I glared at Heilig, but the truth was he was right, I hadn't been completely honest with him, Cukier, Miriam, or Singer. Rumkowski's warning came back to haunt me: "They will hate you when they discover you knew." I still felt like pounding his face with my fists, but the damage was done. Cukier was right, the Nazis had succeeded in making us lose our morals. Each of us could only think of survival, survival at any cost. In my case, it was Regina and Miriam's lives that I convinced myself I wanted Singer to save…but I also wanted him to save my life. I leaned toward Heilig and controlling my anger, I asked, "Were you telling me the truth that you haven't heard from your cousin?"

Heilig nodded. "Oscar decided he'd had enough of the Chairman's ploys and manipulation. He called it, "collaboration," aiding the enemy. I'm not sure what I would call it."

"I don't care about that right now."

"You're right. It doesn't matter. When my idealistic cousin decided there had to be some group somewhere in Poland, fighting the Nazis, he made me apply for his job. He offered to provide information to Neftalin, in exchange for hiring me."

"Neftalin?" That sonofabitch. Another one I couldn't trust. "I wondered why they hired you?" Damn weasel…rat.

Heilig smiled plaintively. "Oscar wanted me to watch over you."

"Watch over me? Spy on me you mean?" I felt my temper about to blow.

"No, of course not. I used the wrong word. Oscar wanted me to protect you…you and Julian."

"You? Protect us? You're afraid of your own shadow!"

Heilig stood. "You know nothing about me. Who do you think introduced Oscar to the Black Market? Why do you think the Germans arrested me...tortured me?" He opened his mouth, and I saw he was missing several teeth. "Yes, I was in their prison because they caught me smuggling drugs."

"You were a drug dealer?"

"No. Oscar and I were sneaking through the barbed wire, running through sewers, risking our lives, to get drugs for the few doctors that remain in the ghetto."

I stared at Heilig and dropped to my chair. "Shit! I didn't know."

"Because I don't smell of the sewer doesn't mean I didn't run through them. You couldn't know. Oscar didn't want you to know. He didn't want your wife to know...to worry."

I still wasn't ready to let down my guard. "You haven't answered. Do you know what happened to Oscar?"

Heilig placed his hands flat on the table and stared hard into my eyes. "I swear on your sweet Regina's life, I do not know what happened to Oscar." He let his voice grow softer. "I truly wish I did. He was more my brother than a cousin." He put his hand on my shoulder, something he'd never done before, something I would never have allowed before. "You should know he told me many times that he loves you."

"No, he loves Miriam...and Regina," I said, finally able to acknowledge the truth.

"No, he loves you. Yes, he loves Miriam, more than anyone he'd ever met. And of course, he loves your darling daughter, who is the miniature of your lovely wife, but if he didn't love you, he would have had no compunction, rascal that he was...is... in taking her away from you." He laughed. "You should know he has no moral compass when it comes to women. Unfortunately for him, he could not bring himself to hurt you. So he left."

I didn't know what to say. "I loved him too." I knew now that was why what he did, what I suspected, had hurt me so deeply.

"I know, or you might have killed him."

I nodded. "Can you help me get Miriam and Regina out of here?" I suddenly felt small and feeble next to him. "Is there anyone who can help?"

Heilig sighed. "I honestly don't know. Oscar was supposed to come back, but..."

"I see."

Heilig turned to his pile of memos. "I will try," he said. "I can't promise anything, but I'll try."

I smiled at him. "That's enough for me. Thank you."

A minute later, a German officer barged through the door.

"Attention!" Heilig shouted, and we both jumped to our feet.

The officer glanced around the room and rushed back outside.

"Please hurry," I said, cracking the door open to see if anything was going on in the hall.

Heilig was already nose-deep into his mail.

The Weasel is back, I thought, doubtful that Singer's cousin, who was nothing like the original, would be able to save us.

CHAPTER 35

J ULY 24, 1942: A MURDER
On July 21, at five o'clock in the afternoon, 55-year-old Chawa Rosenblit was found murdered in her apartment at 9 Ceglana Street. A physician found four fatal head wounds on the victim that had most likely been inflicted by a one-kilogram weight. The incident was immediately reported to officials of the German criminal police, who assumed control for the entire investigation, excluding the ghetto security forces from the case for the time being.

Murder, suicide, death...no reaction anymore. Read about them, summarize, write about them, but feel nothing...I feel nothing. What difference if a woman is bludgeoned to death or starved to death? Is one cause of death worse or better than another? Not to me, the 'numbers man.' But as I read the entry aloud, I thought I saw a strange look on Heilig's face. It had to be my imagination, but why was he looking so morose? A more significant question: why was this particular murder, one of many, of interest to the German police?

Cukier arrived late. Without his usual, "Good morning," he said, "We're all ordered to the Square at 11:00." He then sifted silently through his mail.

I sensed he was still angry. "There is some good news today," I said, hoping to lighten the mood. "The Chairman has begun trade courses at the tailors' workshop for youngsters. The classes will run from 8-4 o'clock and be attended by 300 children in 12 groups." I saw them both look up. "The Chairman says this will create jobs for teachers

175

and instructors. There will also be a dining area which will provide the children meals equivalent to what working people receive in the trade kitchens." I looked at the other two, a forced smile on my face. "That's hopeful, isn't it?"

Cukier aimed a withering look at me. "The Chairman is keeping his promise to protect the children. I hope you see that now?" His tone was icy.

Heilig said, "Julian, nobody doubts the love the Chairman has for children. We all love them. It is difficult not to love our young ones."

Cukier snorted. "You are a bachelor, like your cousin...another playboy, I suppose?"

Heilig was about to respond, but I jumped in. "I was wrong to think that of Oscar, and you are wrong to jump to conclusions about Heilig as well."

Cukier looked angry but remained silent.

I walked toward him. "Julian, I know you are hurt. You are right to feel that way. We have worked together for more than a year, and we are more than co-workers—"

"I thought so too," Cukier interrupted.

"I know." I was grasping for what to say. "We have all kept things from each other, not because we didn't trust each other—"

"Then why? Why did you keep Singer's return a secret from me? You know I'm worried about him. We all are."

I sat in the chair next to Cukier, Rosenfeld's old position. "Do you remember the day you showed us your chest...the letter on it?"

Cukier shifted in his chair.

"You had that letter weeks earlier."

"That was different."

"How was it different? You kept it from us. Why? Why did you do that?"

"I had my reasons. It's different."

"You didn't want us to worry."

Cukier glanced at his handkerchief. "I saw no need to concern you since there was nothing anyone could do."

"And yet, thank God, you are still here. Why is that?"

Cukier looked deep into my eyes. "I wonder that myself."

I pointed my eyes at Heilig. "Tell him."

Heilig looked uneasy.

"I said tell him."

Cukier turned to Heilig. "You did it?"

"My cousin went to Neftalin."

"You told him?" Cukier asked.

Heilig nodded his head.

"Our two young friends have been watching over us," I said, giving Heilig a smile.

Cukier shrugged. "And what did you two have to offer in exchange?"

Heilig almost looked like Singer with that hint of a grin he was famous for. "Information and medicine."

Cukier said, "You wasted your leverage. You only postponed the inevitable. Haven't you gotten it yet? What do you think all the used clothing means?"

"Stop Cukier!"

I looked for the source of the command and saw that Neftalin had entered the room without us knowing.

"Stop speculating about the clothes." Neftalin glared at us. "It is bad enough others listen and spread these depressing falsehoods. Look what I have in my hands." He held up a pile of postcards. "Yes, my friends, we have just received these blessed communications from ghetto residents sent to various labor camps. Apparently, thanks be to God, based on this evidence, all our fears are unfounded."

"May I see those?" I asked.

"Of course. You all may see them to your heart's content. We will spread the word throughout the ghetto. Gentlemen, this should relieve all of our minds."

I examined the cards. "These are fairly extensive writings," I said, expecting the stock sentences and uniform handwriting that might indicate they were forged.

"Do you think we forged them?" Neftalin asked as if reading my mind. "You can read they are all different. Note the variations in handwriting. The contents are generally not of great interest since most deal with family matters, but each is addressed to a specific resident of our community. Just look at them. They are truly a gift in our time of despair."

"What does this one say?" I asked Heilig whose German was superior to mine.

Heilig laughed. "I am receiving such plentiful food here that I would be happy if you, my dear ones, were receiving even anywhere near as much." He knows our ghetto alright," Heilig laughed again.

Neftalin rose. "It's almost eleven. We've all been ordered to meet in the Market Square."

"Is the Chairman making another speech?" Heilig asked, seemingly in no great hurry to join us.

Neftalin glared at him. "Just hurry."

When we reached the town square, we saw the crowd staring to the front.

I gasped. Their eyes were aimed at newly constructed gallows. The wood arms were enough for two to be executed at the same time. Two men were being led up the steps. Their faces were hidden from my view by the crowd of spectators. German soldiers, Gestapo and Kripo, were lined up all around the square, rifle barrels targeting the yellow stars on our chests. Oh my God! They're going to do it, I thought, my legs buckling under me.

In seconds, it was over. Two men, faces hidden by hoods were swinging with broken necks as we were forced to watch. It was the second public execution in the ghetto. I felt faint at the gruesome sight, but also at the thought that one of the men might be my brave, reckless, friend.

It was only after we got back to the conference room that I learned that one man was 45 years old, the other 16. What crime did they commit that merited a public execution? They had escaped from a labor camp near Poznan.

What would be our punishment if we attempted to escape from Lodz? If they executed a 16-year-old in public, what would they do to Miriam and me if we were caught? What would they do to Regina? I had to stop Heilig. He wasn't Singer, and even that mastermind had not been able to come up with an escape plan. For all we knew, he could already be dead, or in prison. There was no way of knowing his fate. As bad as things were in the ghetto, I still believed the war would end soon. All we had to do was hang on a little longer. The Chairman had shown time and time again that he was protecting us.

The men dangled from the gallows, swinging back and forth with the wind.

CHAPTER 36

J **ULY 31, 1942:** THE HORRIFYING MORTALITY RATE
In seven months this year more than 13,000 people have died in the ghetto, whereas in the entire past year, 1941, 11,500 people died, and in 1940, 8,200. Today 95 deaths were registered.

Another month of crushing frustration that nothing was happening. I felt trapped, a rat confounded by blind alleys in an impossible maze. I was paralyzed, conflicted by my fear of trying to escape versus the consequences of remaining. But "the devil you know," so I persisted in sorting through endless reports and attempting to drum up some vestige of passion in our task of reducing all into entries for the Chronicle, which might never be read. I never felt so useless.

Miriam showed stoic resolve in her job, having been sent to a new warehouse at 9 Brzesinska Street. "I'm no longer unloading trucks," she said, a frown on her face. "I sit on a stool at a large table and sort through shoes."

"What do you mean, "sort?"" I asked, grasping for something we could talk about without an argument.

She gave me a meaningful look. "Ben, the shoes are used. There are hundreds and thousands of them."

I remembered Singer's reports. "Are there children's shoes as well?"

She nodded her head, biting her lip.

I stared down at Regina, almost a year old, but because of poor nourishment, so tiny she looked like a fragile little doll. How could I protect her? How could I best give her a chance for life?

The next morning, I again cornered Heilig.

"You must be patient. We are working on it, but our old methods are no longer successful."

When I pressed him for what these methods were, he said, "The less you know, the safer you and your family are."

I recalled that he had claimed to have been tortured by the Kripo and understood his desire to protect us by not revealing his, and the underground's secrets. Singer told me he'd been smuggled in under a load of sewing machines. Now, every time I read a manifest that such machines, or anything, was brought into the ghetto, I hoped for word from him. None came.

"I refuse to write this!" Heilig broke my train of thought.

Cukier was late, so I was in charge. "What are you going on about now?" I asked, still easily annoyed by him.

"They want us to write about shit!"

I examined the memo from the Economics Department. It described the terrible difficulties in removing excrement from the cesspools. "It really is about shit," I said, and irrationally burst into laughter. "We're writing shit about shit!"

Heilig burst into laughter too.

Cukier entered. Seeing us laughing like idiots, he demanded to know what was so funny.

"We're writing shit about shit!" I said and burst into more laughter that was bitter and borne of frustration. I handed him the sheet from the sanitation department head.

He read it silently. "You two idiots don't realize how important excrement issues are," he began, but couldn't control his laughter either. He laughed and coughed, wheezed, at the same time.

All three of us were sitting in our dungeon and laughing our asses off at the irony of having to write commentary about the problems of removing excrement from the ghetto. As it turned out, this was a life-threatening issue, since we had few wagons, no horses. The heavy vehicles we still had were pulled by teams of exhausted prisoners, including young women. The overflowing cesspools and excrement in the streets harbored disease, but in our desperate need for anything that could make us laugh, writing about shit was a trigger.

Our laughter did not last long. Eventually, each of us realized there was nothing funny about our desperate situation. Cukier said he would write the article since "you two are obviously unable to take this critical issue seriously." He was right. As he wrote, "The most painstaking attention should be given to this problem, for here the dry statistics are both eloquent and horrifying." He looked at me and continued aloud, "To replace a draft horse is beyond human power, causing a mortality rate that is a record. Engineer, here are some numbers for you. Last year there were 250 cesspool cleaners, now there are less than 120. Last week alone, six cesspool cleaners died of complete exhaustion while 12 were sent to the hospital. Last year there were 30 wagons, this year 20 at most. It is not a laughing matter."

He was right. The numbers did stop my laughter. There really was nothing funny about humans taking the part of draft horses, pulling heavy wagons loaded down with human shit. "I'm sorry, Julian," I said, "I guess we needed a laugh."

He waved his hand as if to dismiss my concern. His handkerchief was stained with blood. Were the stains darker, larger? His illness was getting worse. "I met with Neftalin this morning," he said between hacking.

The way he said that warned me more bad news was coming.

Cukier gave me a strange look as if focused on some distant scene. "The Deputy confirmed rumors you may have heard about the Warsaw ghetto."

Everyone had been talking about Warsaw, but most people believed the incredible stories were malicious rumors by sick minds eager to spread anxiety, fear, and more depression. I thought the Germans might have been fomenting the rumors to compel even more work from our exhausted bodies. "Are they true?"

"As you know, it is almost impossible to get in and out of our ghetto, so news is hard to come by, impossible to verify." He paused, looking as if he'd lost a loved one. "According to reliable reports, 10,000 people per day have been taken from the Warsaw ghetto."

"10,000 each day?" How could this be true?

Cukier sniffled. "From what we've learned, none of it confirmed, after the resistance was crushed…it never had a chance, the ghetto was evacuated block by block. Everyone was forced from their homes." He paused, glancing at the door. "Tragic incidents occurred."

"How many were deported in total?" I asked, still unable to fathom how 10,000 people could be rousted from their homes and evacuated from the ghetto each day. The sheer logistics of such a massive action presented insurmountable problems which my engineer brain could not imagine the Germans being able to solve.

"Our best information is that forty thousand were removed in the first four days and that the deportations are continuing."

"Warsaw? Our largest population? It is incredible."

Cukier handed me his report. "Perhaps the Germans will be so occupied by events in Warsaw that they will leave us alone."

Heilig leaned toward me. There were tears in his eyes as he whispered, "The last I heard, Oscar was in Warsaw during the uprising."

CHAPTER 37

MONDAY, AUGUST 3
On August 1, 1942, there were 101,259 people living in the ghetto. 2,025 died in the month of July.

I did not tell Miriam about Warsaw, nor that Singer might be dead, or had been swept up in the decimating resettlement of ten thousand Jews per day that was savaging our oldest and largest Jewish community. That had come as a shock to all of us. It reaffirmed my faith that the Chairman had taken the right course in making our ghetto invaluable to the Germans. July had not seen any resettlements here thanks to the Eldest of the Jews employing nearly 80,000 of us in his web-work of factories, workshops, offices, and, of course, the warehouses where Miriam continued to sort clothing.

While the food situation was desperate, most of us were relieved that the police were not going from street to street, house to house, dragging people out for deportation as they had in Warsaw. I watched the reports warily but was being lulled into believing the worst was over. Warsaw satisfied the wolves' appetite for Jewish laborers.

German inspectors, no longer announcing their visits, pounced on our offices and workshops at will. A recent requisition order from Berlin had been gratefully received by the Chairman, and he hurriedly established a telephone manufacturing factory. We were all in awe at how quickly and efficiently he could create a new, or redirect, a factory to meet the German's demands. We believed the more work orders our factories received, the more of us that were employed, the less likely we would face Warsaw's cruel fate. Hunger, exhaustion, death, were constant companions, but there was a growing sense of optimism that so long as we worked, we were safe. We all knew the war had to end at some point, hopefully, soon.

Captives in our department, our small crew was chained to our piles of memos and departmental reports. When we received something unusual, something that drew our faltering attention, we no longer debated its meaning, but noted it and passed it on. There were rare exceptions. A snippet of news might provide inappropriate humor, but we were drowning men gasping for anything that might break the darkness of our precarious existence within the four walls of our cell.

"It's happened again," Heilig said. "They're having internment problems. The Germans should stop us from dying; then there would be no problem."

Cukier coughed. "You should go right up to Hitler and offer this solution to him. Give us decent food, and we will live longer, so all your internment problems will be over."

"Yes, great idea. Like the Germans care that our corpses remain unburied for days?" I burst into laughter. "According to the last count, there are 140 cemetery workers. Hey Germans, we need far more of these valiant burial technicians, or we'll refuse to die."

"We should tell the Chairman. Maybe he'll hire more grave workers for us. He owns the cemetery service too." Heilig said. "He owns everything, from womb to tomb."

Cukier frowned but remained silent.

"The Germans should be told that the cemetery workers are so exhausted and sick that they're dying off and adding to the long lines to get in," I said, laughing at something that in any other situation would not be at all humorous.

Cukier wasn't laughing. "The problem is horses."

I was startled by his comment since Julian, weakened by his progressive illness, now rarely spoke. I marveled how he persisted in appearing for work, but understood the reason.

Cukier's brow, now gray, furrowed as he explained. "The authorities gave the funeral services a few horses, but they are unfit for work. The horses that were a little sturdy, not bony, replacements, they took for themselves."

"So, the solution is well-fed, healthy horses for starving and sickly workers. Makes sense to me," Heilig said.

"So, who will present our solution to the Chairman?" I asked. "I elect Heilig."

"For what?" Neftalin asked, having entered the door without knocking. "What were you discussing? I could use some humor these days." He sat down. "All I get are problems and complaints from all sides."

Cukier answered in his croaking voice. "We were analyzing the current issues in the internment industry."

Neftalin frowned. "I suppose that is humorous in a macabre way."

"I concluded that horses are the solution," Cukier said.

"Actually, the Chairman has set his creative juices to resolving this issue," Neftalin replied.

"Really?" I wondered what our esteemed leader had come up with now. Was he creating a factory to dispose of bodies? I could see it now: thousands of young Jews seated at tables, passing corpse after corpse down a factory line. I could visualize the sharp-toothed hand- saws cutting away limbs, a violation of Jewish law: No man can destroy what God creates. So, what were the sawing noises? I had to shake myself out of such a horror-story image.

Neftalin sighed. "Julian is right about the horses being part of the problem."

Cukier smiled. "For once, I'm right?"

Neftalin continued, "We have no way to transport all the dead, so bodies have been ordered to remain in their homes until they can be picked up."

"Bodies have been ordered?" Heilig shrugged his shoulders. "I hope they listen to the Chairman's orders better than—"

"Heilig," Cukier hissed.

"Wait a minute? This is serious. Bodies are to remain in houses in this terrible heat?" I could almost smell the decaying corpses. "For how long? I pray nobody in our building will elect to die until this proclamation is rescinded." I exaggerated wriggling my nose at an awful odor.

"My God, the stench!" Heilig blurted. "It is bad enough when people die in the streets, but in a cramped and stuffy flat?" He looked at us with stern eyes. "Nobody better die here! That is my order!"

Cukier glared at him.

Neftalin stifled a laugh. Perhaps he was as desperate for some laughter, as we were. "The Chairman has ordered, due to the shortage of hearses—something even Julian did not consider—that new flat wagons will be used to transport the dead. They will carry as many as 30 corpses in one run."

"Run? With 30 corpses, these nags will be lucky if they crawl on their bony knees to the cemetery." Heilig said.

Neftalin handed a thin sheet of paper to Cukier. "Enough humor. The authorities have ordered the shut-down of the outpatient clinic at 17 Zgierska Street. Here is the official decree. It will be made into a factory to help fulfill their orders." He shook his head and left the room.

"Another medical facility closed?" Cukier said. "Soon there will be none left."

"The Germans just want more business for the cemetery," Heilig said. "But wait! Didn't they want to dig it up and put up a new factory there too?"

I'd lost interest in the no longer humorous dialogue. My mind was fixed on the flat wagons that would be carrying all those bodies, piled one on top of the other, on its mournful trip to the cemetery. I could hear the tired, bony horse, asking, "When will these Jews stop dying so I can take a breather?" And the Chairman replies, "Work, work, horse, or you will be turned into sausage, a rare delight for starving bellies." I shook myself back to reality and said, "I think I'm going insane. I just heard a horse talking to our Chairman."

Heilig hissed, "That's like a horse talking to a jackass!"

Cukier shot him a sharp look and then glanced at the door.

I thought Heilig's comment was funny and wished I could repeat it to Miriam, but knew she wouldn't laugh. She was keeping too much inside her. She no longer even confided in me about the small wads of bills, jewelry, ragged papers, and the few I.D. cards she ran across each day in the sorting house. I think she realized there was no escape for us, no secret plan, no white knight to come to our rescue. Whatever she was thinking, she kept to herself. Even as we celebrated Regina's first birthday, I felt the wall between us was insurmountable. I saw it in her eyes. Those once-beautiful eyes were cold and bitter. My only hope was that the bombs would soon fall, and all of this nightmare would be blown to confetti.

CHAPTER 38

T UESDAY, AUGUST 11, 1942
For several days a group of 50 policemen has been leaving each morning by order of the German authorities and returning late at night. They supervise the disposal of goods belonging to the Jews driven from the town of Pabianice. It is not known where the belongings, clothing, bedding, and furniture they left behind will be sent.

I looked at my entry of August 7th and thought how wonderful it would have been if, on the date of Regina's first birthday, we'd gotten word that the Germans had been defeated and the war was over. Instead, we got more misery. The depth of our suffering was without a bottom. Starvation dispelled any positive news, of which there was only the flow of orders from the military.

It was the latest army requisitions that were a clue as to how things were going for Hitler: white shirts, pants and hooded caps with drawstrings. We called them the winter uniforms. They were grey on the reverse. Every workshop was placed on emergency shifts to produce several hundred thousand of these white camouflage suits.

"Why would they need so many snowsuits unless they are in trouble in Russia?" I asked.

Heilig spat, "That would be too much to hope for."

Cukier smiled benignly.

At first, I thought his mind had drifted away. He did that quite a bit lately. One second, he would be with us, his usual insightful way, and in the next, his eyes would take on a glaze. He would remain incommunicado for painfully long minutes. I felt great concern during these gaps, even though he looked happy. It was as if his brain was taking a brief, well-earned, vacation. "Julian," I prodded. "Julian?"

"I was thinking of Napoleon," he said, his voice sounding detached. "Are you students of history? If Hitler were, he would have avoided Russia like the plague."

Heilig nodded. "Is that what you think is happening to the Nazis now?"

I envisioned our white uniforms being stripped from a million frozen, dead, German soldiers. I could pray for an endless field of naked corpses standing like bizarre icicles stretching from the Polish border to Moscow. "It would be wonderful if history did repeat itself," I said.

Cukier nodded. "I fear it is too late for our friends in Pabianice and Warsaw. Oh God! Warsaw? Why? Why?" Tears burst from his eyes.

I rushed toward him and held his head against my chest. He didn't push me away but sobbed uncontrollably as if a dam had broken after months of pressure.

I had escaped from our room yesterday and headed for the Central Prison. I was eager to hear news from Warsaw but found less than 200 Jews from Pabianice. I surveyed the lost and sad remnants. There were only a few women, five or six children. When I tried to find out what happened, a man burst into tears and said, "We are the last Jews from our town. There are no more."

I turned to another man. "What happened to your children?" I had to know. It was why I had risked going there, risked encountering Gestapo, who had increased their presence on our streets.

The man tearfully replied, "We had examinations…German doctors. They stamped letters on us." He showed me a large A on his chest. "The weak, the elderly…our children…those in category "B" were sent elsewhere." He looked at me. "Do you know where they are? Please, tell me you know?"

I was used to this narrative by now. "I'm sorry, my friend, we don't know anything more than you do."

He shook his head and asked again, "So you know where they are?"

I walked away. Seeing the bedraggled, confused, mournful souls in that prison was too much to bear. I had hoped for a kernel of good news. There was none.

As I walked back to the offices at the Balut Market, I heard a wagon approaching. I stopped to look at it, a kind I had never seen before. It was pulled by a horse who looked as if he were on his last legs. The driver was seated at the front of the large vehicle which was constructed of wood planks and with two doors on top. Several men were walking behind as it moved slowly down muddy roads. I guessed its task but still followed. Why? I don't know. Everything else I'd become indifferent to…except for my Regina, and now this ungainly wagon.

A woman was standing by a doorway on Zgierska street. She had her hands to her side, and her face showed no emotion as she directed the three men trailing the wagon to enter the building. She remained outside, her face without color, without any expression of life. When the men emerged from the doorway, they were carrying a body wrapped in a sheet. "Do you wish to say anything to him?" One of the carriers asked.

The woman glanced at the carrier, but no words escaped her parched lips.

A worker climbed up the back of the wagon on its thin slats. He and the driver pulled open the twin doors on the top. The two men on the ground braced themselves and hurled the body on top of what looked like twenty or more corpses. Without words, the men lowered the doors and followed on foot as the death wagon lumbered away.

I remained rooted in place. They didn't even paint it, I found myself thinking irrationally, as I wondered if someday a wagon such as this would carry away my body.

When I returned to our safe haven, I wrote my entry about the last Jews of Pabianice. My mind kept returning to the makeshift hearse and all the bodies thrown inside its unfinished wood stomach. I leaned over to Heilig and whispered, "Any news from Warsaw?"

He grimaced. "It's not good. The Germans are punishing everyone for the rebellion. Deportations are continuing. The rumors are that by the end of the month there will be no Jews left."

"That's not what I meant."

Heilig whispered, "There is nothing."

CHAPTER 39

FRIDAY, AUGUST 21, 1942: REMOVALS OF FIGURES AND CROSSES
By order of the authorities, the figure of Christ was removed from its pedestal in front of the Church of the Most Blessed Virgin Mary on Zgierska Street. They also cut down four large wooden crosses in the courtyard and a figure at 17 Zgierska.

"Maybe they're tired of tormenting only Jews," Heilig said.

"They hate all religion," Cukier responded. "How else can they do such bestial things? I'm convinced the Nazis are creations of Satan. Hitler is the devil himself."

At the word devil, I thought of how I'd thought of Rumkowski as the Satan of the ghetto. That was before I became one of those in the "inner circle." In all the time I'd been employed by the Eldest of the Jews, I had not made up my mind about this question. Every day we were bombarded by bad news, and ominous rumors, but our Chairman, though battered and no longer in charge, still traversed the ghetto in his coach. He inspected his factories, prodding us to work, work, work, produce, produce, produce, and serving himself up as the symbol of our hope for survival. We were mindful that the Lodz ghetto could be the last surviving bastion of Jewish culture and that thousands of years of proud history rested in the Eldest of the Jews' hands. Everything depended on his ability to cope with all the terrible decisions the Germans kept forcing on him. Was he a saint? Was he the devil? It didn't matter. We were alive. That was what I kept in mind as each day it became more difficult to deal with my task. "The Chairman has it much worse than we do," I told myself. So, I was able to write about ten suicides a day, five shootings near the barbed wire, dozens of deaths from hunger, disease, and exhaustion. Even when the following entry crossed my path, it no longer made a significant impression. We had become hardened, all "numbers men."

AN EXTRACT FROM THE DEATH RECORDS
  1. Tusk, Machla Golda age 17 died July 10, 1942 (daughter)
  2. Tusk, Chaim Kasriel age 22 died July 26, 1942 (son)
  3. Tusk, Cywia age 45 died August 11, 1942 (mother)
  4. Tusk, Majer age 47 died July 28, 1942 (father)

Still alive:
  Tusk, Abram age 21
  Tusk, Rywka age 15

"How did they die?" Cukier asked after I showed him the entry.
  "It doesn't say."
  "So why include them?"
  "I found it interesting. It's all one family."
  "But you don't know how they died."
  "No. It doesn't say."
  "Why don't you find out?"
  "Why?"
  "Because you said it was interesting."
  "What difference does it really make?"
  "None. But you chose to include it."
  "Only because it is indicative of what is happening here." Julian was irritating me. "We know nothing about who they were, what they did, and what killed them. The most important thing about their lives is that they all died in the same brief period. Isn't that ironic?"
  Cukier nodded. "If they hadn't they would barely merit a footnote."

He lifted his hand, studying his fingers. "What will I merit? How will any of us be remembered once our stay on this sad planet is ended?"

Heilig chuckled. "We'll be invisible men. Nobody will know much at all about our lives...the lives of the writers of this worthless pile of toilet paper...not even signed...except for the few you initial B.O."

Cukier smiled. "It is ironic that while our words may be clues for the future...if any Jews survive. Warsaw? I never dreamed I'd see the day that center of Jewish life would vanish....I must stay on track. If any Jews survive, they will find our work...but we? The writers. Nothing. You are right, Heilig, we will become invisible. Only men like our leader, Chairman Rumkowski...and Hitler, who never should have been born, will become famous, or infamous, depending on how this war ends."

"It is all about how history will judge them," I said.

"Yes, how history will judge," Cukier said. "And God. I would not want to be in Hitler's shoes when God sets his hand upon his miserable soul."

I found it difficult to believe that a man of Cukier's intellect could still place trust in this uncaring God, a myth from our ancient past. How could he believe in this God who was unable to feel sympathy for our suffering? "I suppose it is better to believe in a deity, than not believe in anything but the humanity of man. Amen," I said.

Heilig laughed.

"What's so funny?"

Heilig waved my report. "Four members of one family die within a month of each other. In a pulp mystery, one would blame the survivors killing them to inherit. But there is no inheritance here. The Nazis have it all. Isn't that funny? There is nothing of wealth to serve as a motive for these murders by the Germans. That, my friends, is hysterical."

"Food would be a unique motive for your murders. "Starving wife kills husband and family to steal ration cards!" Turn the pages for the exciting end..."

"I think we'd best get back to work," Cukier said.

"Oy!" Heilig exclaimed, holding up a sheet of paper.

"Now what?" I asked, fearful of more bad news.

"The Chairman is at it again."

"What do you mean?" I leaned back, freed from my typing.

"He's ranting about crime again, thefts in workshops, distribution points, bakeries, and in kitchens!" Heilig gave me a wicked look. "The rats did it."

"You're an idiot," Cukier said, using his favorite word to describe our penchant for finding humor in the humorless news.

"What is he proposing this time?" I asked. "Shall we dig out the guillotine?"

"You're close. "More severe punishments." He says otherwise there will be "dire consequences" and you know what that means?"

All three of us said at once, "The Germans."

Heilig whistled. "Wow! He's really getting tough. He says anyone who does not report crimes or hides the perpetrators will receive the same harsh punishments as the evil-doers."

"And what else can he do to punish us?" I asked, skeptical that any punishment could eradicate the rampant crime and pilfering by our starving people.

"He's ordered a special solitary section in our prison. All violators sent there will have no visitors, reduced rations, and lose the right to work. And we know what that means." He mimed hanging himself.

"Good for him," Cukier said. "If he doesn't stop these criminals the Gestapo will descend on us like vultures."

"They're already picking at our flesh like vultures," Heilig said.

I thought of Miriam. She'd gotten into the habit of bringing a scattering of items she smuggled in from the warehouse. She thought I didn't know, but I'd seen her placing some trinkets beneath a plank hidden from view under our bed. She looked like a squirrel socking away nuts. I saw little of value when I examined her cache, so I let it go, hoping she would tire of this game. Frightened she'd eventually be caught, I demanded she stop before she got caught.

"One of us must be prepared," she replied.

"Prepared for what?"

"To bribe the guards."

Stealing these things wasn't a game. Somewhere in these misbegotten objects, my little thief hoped there might be one, two, or three treasures, that could be bartered for some favor...perhaps for Singer to use as bribes. She still had hope. I had none.

But what if she were caught?

I made up my mind to convince her of the danger of stealing these useless objects from the warehouse, but she refused to listen. The very next day, she brought home a broken toy horse. Regina introduced it to her rag doll. In the shadows of the candle-lit room, the smile on my daughter's lips provided a tiny light.

Watching Regina provided me a rare sense of peace. Miriam was on the floor playing with her. She wasn't arguing with me. I closed my eyes. Being invisible was good. Would death feel like this?

CHAPTER 40

T UESDAY, AUGUST 25, 1942
*The hottest day of the year. The temperature reached 42 degrees.
(Centigrade) The threat of typhus has resulted in proclamations
concerning cleanliness.*

God punished us with so much already, so why this? After suffering the cold winter, August brought a heat wave. Word came that the lack of water and the warm temperatures, followed by an enormous invasion of caterpillars, had destroyed our cabbage crop. Only the skeletons of leaves and stalks remained. I witnessed the frenzied efforts to clean up the mess and rush the replanting to relieve the terrible hunger that was killing us. The whiplash of the punishing heat wave made any efforts useless.

A man, hat in hand, lamented, "I've never seen such an invasion of caterpillars in my life."

"Can't they be cleared off?" I asked, astonished by the destruction.

"They came too quickly and suddenly. We were too late. It is the ten plagues again. It is because of *him*." He looked at me. "You won't report me?"

"No. Have no fear."

"It doesn't really matter. I thought we could grow a little to set aside, but the plague of caterpillars…" He let out a deep sigh. "I suppose it was meant to be."

I left him in the dirt examining the hordes of caterpillars. We Jews are all fatalists at heart. We've suffered so much, survived so much, over thousands of years. What is a horde of caterpillars compared to all that?

When I told Cukier of the plague of caterpillars, he laughed bitterly and said, "Once the cabbages are gone, the caterpillars too will starve to death."

I hadn't thought of that.

Heilig added his own bit of warped humor: "Once the Jews are gone, who will the Nazis have to persecute? Maybe they'll all die too?"

Cukier snarled, "The Jews will never be gone. Never. Do you understand? You, and I, even the Engineer—although he, being so damn logical, will most likely outlive us all—we may not survive this, but Jews will always live. Maybe someday in the promised land? Maybe someday only in America where the smartest Jews already are thriving? But we will survive." He burst into a terrible fit of coughing.

I wanted to calm him, so I said, "You're right. Jews will always survive."

Cukier raised himself from his chair, but the coughing knocked him back down again.

I hurried to Neftalin's office to get water. I banged on the Deputy's door. There was no answer. I had to have water for Julian, so I pushed inside. The pitcher was on Neftalin's desk. I could not help myself... the document was a magnet. It was in Neftalin's distinctive handwriting: "Pabianice, Belchatow, Ozorkow, Zelow, Wielun, Strykow, Sieradz, Lask, Warsaw...they are all empty...being emptied...the process continues." I wanted to look away, but farther down he'd written, "When will they target us? Are we truly safe?"

I forgot the water and rushed from the office. I was shaken by the Deputy putting in print the dread that was a meat cleaver hanging over all of us. He had been so assured...a rock. What could I believe in? What hope was left to us?

Singer had urged us to fight. Was it still possible? We'd heard that Warsaw had rebelled against the Nazis and the rebels had been brutally crushed. All the residents were punished with deportation and the destruction of this hallowed bastion of Jewish culture. We Jews could not crush caterpillars, but the Nazis could send three hundred thousand Warsaw Jews, to parts unknown, in a month. Incredible! Impossible to believe. But Neftalin's note erased any doubt. Warsaw was no more. Was Lodz next?

I returned to our quarters, unsure of what to divulge to my friends.

Heilig was attempting to type at our tyrannical machine. "I do not know how you manage this. I swear the German sadists must have invented it."

"Where is Julian?"

His chair was empty, briefcase gone.

Heilig placed his hand on my shoulder. "My friend, his coughing is worse. There is no medicine. I'm surprised every day when he shows up. He's determined. I'll say that for him."

I pushed his hand away. I was in no mood to argue and tell him that Julian was one of the bravest men I'd ever met. Yes, we disagreed about certain things, particularly about the Eldest of the Jews. He still perceived the Chairman as a savior, to be trusted and given unwavering loyalty. I was worried we had taken the wrong route, and Singer had been right when he argued we should be fighting Germans, not supplying their military. Despite that conflict, Cukier had earned my affection and respect. Now, weakened by illness and lack of nourishment, he was not the robust man I'd met only a year and a half ago. Heilig had never seen the original, the whole man that Cukier had been. He could not understand all my friend had accomplished. I did not have the strength nor resolve to educate our Weasel. Rosenfeld would have had that patience, but where was he? I clutched the pipe bowl in my pocket.

"I thought you were going for water?" Heilig asked.

I could not tell him what I'd read. I was drained. "You have not heard from our mutual friend?" I asked again. Had anyone in our ghetto heard from anyone outside? Only rumors and the terrifying stories of the newcomers penetrated the quarantine the Germans had successfully placed around us. In hushed, frightened, voices, the dazed immigrants gasped out narratives too painful to believe. Tear-filled eyes were evidence of families violently separated. Some sent here, but women, the weak, elderly, and children, selected to go to places unknown. I interviewed so many of these ghostly immigrants. Their histories were remarkably the same: rousted out of their homes with only the clothing on their backs; standing in the street until marched to some assembly point, always uncertain of their fate. And, of course, the shock, their greatest fear realized...their children ripped away from them. I saw the dull eyes on exhausted, confused, faces, turn up to me, and with quivering lips force up the words, "Do you know where our children are?"

How could I tell them what I now believed happened to their loved ones? How could I tell them that my own wife, my Miriam, was one of the hundreds sorting clothes, hats, and even underpants... all with ripped seams and torn pockets? How could I reveal our suspicions about the endless stream of trucks filled with shoes, all sizes...baby shoes...missing heels and soles...all being examined and sorted? How could I tell them what I could not comprehend, could not accept, though the evidence was undeniable? How the Germans could manage this, the enormity of this atrocity, if it was true, defied logic, was unprecedented in human history. So, I still fought what I now knew was the most likely reality. I hid my fear and replied, "No, my friend, we know as little as you." Then I escaped.

Back in our dungeon, when I wrote the required entries after these interviews, I could no longer conceal the suspense tormenting us. The not knowing the fate of those we cared about, Singer, Rosenfeld, Miriam's parents, my parents, tainted every day of sunshine as summer drew to a close.

When I walked home that day, unable to put Neftalin's note out of my brain, I kept a wary eye for the police and the zombies. Even the workers, starving and losing hope, were shadows of their former selves, pale, directionless. We were ghosts, without little more than the instinctive drive for survival keeping us alive.

Miriam didn't come to greet me when I entered our flat. She was on the floor playing with Regina. "Not in your mouth, Gina," she said, pulling some object away.

It was a tiny doll.

"Gina, I said, not in your mouth," she shouted, pulling the doll away again.

I expected an outcry from the baby, but there was none. When we played hide-and-seek, before her bedtime, Regina remained under the coverlet, hidden by a pile of soiled clothing, in the closet.

"You mustn't move," I said, hovering near, assuring she remained still and silent. "No laughing, Regina. Stay still so Daddy can't find you."

She was allowed to giggle when I made a big show of finding her. As a reward for her being a good girl, I swung her around and around and laughed with her. It was a rare delight to hear her laugh like a normal child. She was becoming quite good at playing dead.

Miriam watched our game silently, never joining in. I didn't mind. I felt no passion, no attachment, to her, to this life. I recalled Miriam's words the night we made love: "How can we bring a child into a world such as this?" Then I looked at Regina. I felt tears in my eyes as I fought the temptation to provide the answer to her question. I had the means. If I could do it, the three of us, all at once, we would be news on everyone's lips. "How could he do such a thing?" "It was an act of evil and cowardice." "He killed his wife and child?" I had thought anyone who contemplated suicide was insane. When I read of someone ingesting pills, rat poison, hanging themselves, throwing themselves from high windows and roofs, I had believed it was wrong. Rosenfeld said, "It is a sin to destroy what God makes beautiful and sacred." But now, witnessing my wife and child withering away in this slow death, I didn't know the answer to Miriam's question. My baby was playing with a dead child's home-made doll.

Regina crawled into my lap. I wondered what her eyes were asking.

I responded with a smile and enfolded her in my arms. I'd protect her until this war ended. It will end soon. It must end soon. "Sweetheart, let's play hide-and-seek with daddy?"

CHAPTER 41

T UESDAY, SEPTEMBER 1, 1942: PATIENTS EVACUATED
Yesterday evening the authorities demanded that a delegation
of 50 policemen be sent to Balut Market at 5 o'clock this morning.

The Chairman added a new member to our group, Jozef Zelkowcz, a college professor. At first, I thought Rosenfeld had returned. He could have been the Doctor's twin except for his unkempt appearance, white hair, long and stringy. He also never rubbed his hands from the cold. I knew nothing else about him. I no longer wanted to know, nor to make friends with any of these men who might vanish at any moment. When I saw this stranger, my hand clutched the bowl of my old friend's pipe.

I interrupted Zelkowicz's reading of his entry. "They've been doing this for weeks, to assist in the vacating of Jews from apartments in nearby towns."

Jozef grunted. "This is different."

Heilig sighed. "I prefer the routine."

Cukier stared at his hands.

Zelkowicz continued, "You are right, Bernard, the police have been used in this way, but this time the police were ordered to Wesolo Street."

I felt a chill. "The hospital again?"

Cukier's voice was flat. "What happened?"

Zelkowicz read on. "All the patients were evacuated."

I imagined the scene. Panicked, helpless patients, being forced from their beds, screaming, terrified, not understanding—thrown into trucks. "What about the staff?" I asked.

"The night staff was there, but the doctors and day staff were kept out by the Germans. The streets were cordoned off. That why they wanted our police."

I didn't know what else to ask.

Heilig asked, "Where did the trucks take them all?"

"It wasn't over," Jozef said.

"What do you mean, it wasn't over?" I asked.

"They drove the trucks to four other hospitals."

"They emptied them all in one night?" Heilig asked.

Zelkowicz nodded. "So it says."

"The children's hospital on Lagiewnicka Street?" I asked, praying at least they had been spared.

"All."

"All?" I felt sick. Not the children? Please, not them?

"Some patients tried to escape. The Order Service, with the authorities closely observing, chased them down." He sighed. "Most were dragged into the trucks, kicking and screaming…some were beaten by clubs…and then thrown into the trucks."

"Those poor people," I muttered.

Cukier nodded.

Heilig again asked, "Where did the trucks take them?"

Zelkowicz shook his head.

"Are they in the ghetto still?" I asked, remembering the rumors surrounding the previous evacuation of the hospital.

"No. They are gone."

Heilig jumped from his chair. "Where is the Chairman when this is happening to us? He swore to protect them! He swore to protect us all!"

"Stop it! Shouting will attract attention," I said, trying to shove him back into his chair. I glanced at the door. "They are everywhere these days. It is not as before. We must be careful."

"Get your hands off me! It's time you see the truth. The devil can't protect us! This is just the beginning."

"Shut up! Sit down and shut up!" I pressed Heilig down hard, but he pushed himself free. "All those poor patients...those poor souls. They don't even understand what happened."

"They're better off," Cukier said softly.

His lack of emotion surprised me. "How can they be better off?"

Cukier asked, "Do we know where the Chairman was?"

Zelkowicz shook his head.

Cukier rose to his feet. He looked unsteady as he approached Heilig. "Go sit down. We are all upset." He picked up his cane and left the room.

Heilig returned to his seat. He grabbed his pen and began to write.

I wondered where Julian went but was still too stunned by the terrible news, I envisioned the scene of frightened patients leaping out of windows and being chased and tackled by our police. "I can't imagine how their relatives must feel, waking up to this news," I said.

Heilig stood. "I'll go check the hospital and see what is happening," he said in a much calmer voice.

"No, you won't," I ordered. "You could be taken too."

He turned. "Do I look insane?"

I would have laughed at that, thinking we were all insane, sitting and writing endless notes while the ghetto was collapsing around us. I tried to be patient. "It isn't safe. The Germans will grab up anyone if they so choose."

Heilig remained standing, looking undecided.

Julian returned and sat down. "Henryk said the Chairman was in the hospital on Drewnowska Street since early morning." He smiled sadly. "The Deputy said the Chairman did everything humanly possible to negotiate with the authorities."

Heilig muttered, "It didn't help."

"Neftalin said the trucks had already left the ghetto. There was nothing that could be done."

My engineer brain would not be denied. "Why would the Germans do this? Why now? Why in such haste?"

Cukier replied. "Neftalin said Rumkowski had no inkling of this action. He can't even express an opinion as to why it happened." He shivered. "Engineer, dear friend, they're all in shock." He leaned his cane against the wall.

Heilig said, "They want everything, even our cemetery, to become their factories, part of their war machine."

Cukier shook his head and replied, "I asked. Henryk had no answers. He said the Chairman was totally taken off-guard and was dealing with the distraught relatives." He wiped his mouth with his cloth. "The Deputy had just returned from Wesolo Street and said he had never heard so much crying and despair. He appeared genuinely shaken. I've never seen him like this."

I imagined how I would feel if my relatives, my child, who I had placed in the care of the hospital, was snatched away by force.

Cukier held up a stack of papers. "Life goes on."

Zelkowicz handed me his report. I began to type, almost as much a machine as the hated typewriter. I paused after typing the last paragraph he'd written:

"But meanwhile, life goes on. Wagons of potatoes are arriving, overshadowing other concerns. Anyone who has not been directly affected thinks of tomorrow, believing that fate may protect him from new trials. People's minds have been blunted—the stomach rules over everything! Sad, painful, but, unfortunately, true!"

"Life goes on...as long as the stomach is filled." Zelkowicz writes well, I reflected, but I was tired of it all. I kept typing. It kept me from thinking. Keep hitting the keys. Keep hitting the keys. Keep hitting the damn keys....

CHAPTER 42

SEPTEMBER 2, 1942: LITTZMANNSTADT-GETTO
All yesterday, day and night, the populace was affected by nightmarish experiences...

I admired Zelkowicz's writing. He had a way of expressing emotions I had lost or never had. In one sentence, he captured the mood of the ghetto after news of the hospital evacuation hammered home our precarious situation.

"I like your writing," I said to Jozef.

"Thank you."

The door opened.

We stood, prepared to salute our oppressors. We never knew when they would come to inspect our room. When they did, Cukier, acting healthier than he was, would stand with us and nod affirmatively as Neftalin described how our record-keeping was saving the Reich money. The authorities would sneer at us, Jewish intellectuals, whose only saving grace was aiding their supply chain. A few shakes of their heads, more contemptuous looks, and as abruptly as they invaded, they stormed out. We never knew if we would exist for another day. We never knew when they would return, so when the door opened, we stood to save our lives.

Neftalin leaned his back against the wall by our door. "The authorities have ordered the Eldest of the Jews to hand over all those who fled the hospital."

"You're kidding?" I exclaimed.

Neftalin shook his head. "They have selected the arbitrary number of 200. The Order Service has been issued strict orders to round up the hospital escapees who are in hiding or to arrest members of their families if they fail to determine where the escapees are."

"They're going to take family members?" Heilig asked. "Can't the Chairman stop this madness?"

Neftalin looked as if he'd swallowed a lemon as he continued. "There have been some tragic events associated with this action by the authorities. A wife was taken instead of her hospitalized husband. Sadly, we learned later the husband had been taken the day before." He checked his notes. "Also a boy terrified his mother was included in the evacuation, died of a heart attack. The mother was taken anyway." He shook his head. "Nothing we have seen has matched the brutality of this round-up."

I looked at Heilig. When was the Weasel going to do something to help me save Miriam and Regina?

The Weasel looked away.

Neftalin perused his notes. "You will receive a report that a woman fled the hospital the day after the birth of her child. Sadly, the child was stillborn…" He paused, looking miserable, but then continued. "The mother was still on the run. She died today."

"How did she die?" Zelkowicz asked.

Neftalin looked uneasy.

"Do we know how many victims there were?" I asked.

Neftalin sighed. "The exact number of victims cannot be determined." He paused, a pained look on his face. "Some nurses tried to help patients escape. They were fired upon."

"They shot at nurses in the hospital?" I asked.

"Fortunately, none were hit."

What kind of men shoot at nurses?

Neftalin looked to see if there were any more questions.

"Is it over?" I asked.

"Nobody knows. I can tell you the Chairman has been working

tirelessly to terminate these events. Our prayers must be for his success."

Neftalin left, but just before he did, he glanced at me and said, "Be extra careful. The wolves are closing in."

I left early, curious to see the hospital for myself. It was only 10 A.M., but something seemed ominously wrong. The street was blocked by German vehicles. Guards were holding screaming, crying, people back behind wood barricades.

"What is happening?" I asked a woman heading away from the barricade.

"The trucks from yesterday are back." She hurried away.

I grabbed the shoulder of another woman, clutching a baby in her arms. "What is going on? Why are the trucks here?"

She glanced at my identification, spit on the ground at my shoes, and with a hostile look into my face, hurried away.

"I'm not your enemy," I said, but she was gone.

I spied the Jewish policeman who I had spoken to before. He was standing behind the crowd, his club in hand. I approached too quickly. The club inched up.

Thankfully, he recognized me. He didn't lower the club.

"What is happening? Why are the trucks back?"

"Are you on government business?" he asked, not removing his eyes from the crowd.

I held up my card.

"The authorities are picking up the last escapees from yesterday." He leaned his head closer. "It is almost over. Be safe. Go home."

It was good advice. I did not want to see the patients' faces as they were forced onto the trucks while their relatives lamented their loss.

At home, I dismissed our sitter, Dorka. She'd heard of the incidents at the hospital the day before and asked if I'd known about it. I had the feeling she would have quit helping us with Regina right then and there if I had answered that I did.

"I swear on my child's life, I did not know. Nobody knew."

Dorka, slightly older than Miriam, but hair gray and matted, smiled with missing teeth. "He knew. That bastard knows it all."

"Who? Who do you think knew?"

"The damn Chairman lets it happen. As long as it doesn't impact on his wife and their greedy family, all is permitted."

I closed my eyes. If only I could have a few minutes of peace? I told myself he did not know about this. Nobody did. This was the Germans, only the Germans. "You can go now," I replied.

She shook her fist. "If I thought you knew—"

I was furious. "Of course not! I didn't. Nobody did."

I was glad when she left. "Come, Regina. Sit on my lap and make me smile?"

Regina crawled over and clambered onto my lap. She pushed her head into my chest, wrapped her fingers around my thumb and lifted it to her mouth. She sucked on it as if it satisfied her hunger. I held her, my eyes fixed on her face until she fell asleep.

When Miriam came home, she reported that the entire workshop had been disrupted by the news of the hospital evacuations. She lowered herself to a chair and studied me for several long minutes before she asked, "Did you know this was going to happen?"

Why did everyone think I knew? I closed my eyes and prayed to God for an end to all this suffering. When I opened my eyes, Miriam was still staring at me. "Do I really have to answer that?"

Miriam didn't move. She wasn't going to show me any mercy.

I was cradling my child, the only treasure I still possessed. Even Miriam was lost to me, doubted me. I felt trapped by her accusatory stare. Violence was seething inside me, but I was holding my child. I hissed, "No, Miriam, I did not know."

Miriam didn't apologize. Perhaps she didn't believe me. I don't know, but I clutched my sleeping child almost as protection from the woman I no longer understood, the wife who no longer trusted me. Rumkowski was right at least about one thing. He warned me others would hate me if they found out I didn't share what I knew. I never guessed it would be my Miriam who would hate me.

CHAPTER 43

L ITZMANNSTADT-GHETTO, SEPTEMBER 14, 1942
The period of September 5-12, 1942, will leave indelible memories among that portion of the ghetto's population on whom fate smiles and who survive the war.

One week, eight days...an eternity.

The square was where I was when it happened. Miriam was thankfully home with Regina. All work in the ghetto was ordered stopped for the day. The crowd was waiting anxiously for the Chairman's speech. Every able-bodied person who was not essential to the operation of the machines clanking in the factories was ordered to attend. Nobody knew the purpose of this assembly. Rumors circulated that the war was not going well for Germany. Japan had drawn America, the sleeping giant, into the fray, and the Russian campaign had turned the white uniforms, most manufactured in our shops, to blood red. Were the rumors correct again? Were the Germans on the run? Was that why we were gathered here awaiting our Chairman's speech? Was it good news at last?

Rumkowski arrived, surrounded by his police and flanked by many of his high officials. I searched Deputy Neftalin's face for clues, but he was staring straight ahead at the gathering throng. German soldiers were ringed around the perimeter. They were, as usual, armed. They reminded me of vultures, cold eyes staring down at us, waiting for some signal to roar down and tear what little flesh we had left from our weary bones.

213

The Chairman removed his familiar hat, and the crowd, desperate for good news, fearing anything else, became silent.

I always found the Chairman's voice harsh, raspy, but its firmness reassuring. Today, he started in an unusually restrained tone. *"A severe blow has befallen the ghetto." He said and paused. "They are asking from it the best it possesses—children and old people."

What was happening? I felt the shock, an earthquake, but what did it mean?

Rumkowski waited for quiet and began again. "I have not had the privilege to have a child of my own, and therefore I devoted the best of my years to children. I lived and breathed together with the children."

I know you love children. Why are you repeating this? We believe you love children. What did you say before? It was a mistake? I heard wrong?

The audience was silent, all eyes on the man in the tweed coat who said, "I never imagined that my own hands would have to deliver the sacrifice to the altar."

Abraham had been ordered by God to sacrifice his son on the altar. Sacrifice? Did everyone else hear what I was hearing?

The voice on the microphone cracked with emotion. "In my old age, I must stretch out my hands and beg: Brothers and sisters give them to me! Fathers and mothers... give me your children..."

I glanced around me, not believing. Many others were staring up at our leader in shock. I heard anguished crying, angry protests, dreadful weeping. It wasn't real. I hadn't heard correctly. Why wasn't I crying? Because I didn't believe it. It was a dream...a nightmare. Wake up! Wake up!

The Chairman shouted into the microphone. "I had the premonition that something was descending upon us. I anticipated something, and I constantly stood on alert like a guard to avoid that something. But I could not do it, because I did not know what was menacing us. I did not know what is awaiting us. That the sick were taken away from the hospitals, this was for me totally unanticipated."

I heard whispers of doubt rising around me. I didn't know. I didn't know, I heard myself silently protesting to the crowd, echoing what I had said to Miriam. Miriam? She didn't believe me. Did I believe him? Had he finally fought for us as he claimed?

The Chairman's voice was pleading. "You have the best sign: I had my own kin and near ones there, and I could not do anything for them. I thought that it would end with this, that after that we would be left in peace. This is the peace for which I yearn so strongly, for which I have always worked and striven, but it turned out that something different was predestined for us." He paused again, staring down at us with sad, exhausted, eyes. "The luck of Jews is of course thus: always to suffer more and worse, particularly in wartime."

"God, how much more can we bear? How much more?" I heard someone behind me cry out. Some were now praying in low voices. There was a constant hum.

I was straining to hear, to understand, waiting for him, our savior, to deny it was real.

Rumkowski continued, "Yesterday, during the day, I was given a command to send twenty-odd thousand Jews out from the ghetto: if not ... 'We will do it.' And the question arose: Should we take it over and do it ourselves, or leave it to others to carry out?"[2]

There it was, the fundamental question: should Jews, under any threat, do the dirty work for the Nazi bastards? This was the question no amount of logic could resolve in my conflicted brain. Singer had

---

[2] This speech, one of the most infamous in history, I decided to include in its entirety, with Ostrowski's imagined reactions as dramatic breaks. I also decided to retain the grammatical errors and inconsistencies of this speech as much as possible.

NOTE: The scenes in the workroom are my imagining of what might have been said when these real events occurred. In a number of instances, I have incorporated language from the entries of The Chronicle of the Lodz Ghetto, as edited and translated by Lucjan Dobroszycki, (Yale University Press, 1984) within the dialogue to ground in reality. I strongly recommend that you read the original Chronicle to learn more about this tragic ghetto and its controversial leader. My main purpose in writing this novel is to make people aware of this remarkable document.

an answer. Ostrowski did not.

Our leader was speaking again. "But being dominated not by the thought, 'How many will be lost,' but by the thought, 'How many can be saved,' we, that is I and my closest co-workers, came to the conclusion that as difficult as this will be for us, we must take into our own hands the carrying out of the decree. I have to carry out this difficult and bloody operation. I must cut off the limbs in order to save the body! I must take children because, if not, others could also, God forbid, be taken…"

Here was our Chairman's answer: If he didn't do this terrible thing, the Germans, ferocious, brutal, bound by no conscience, no moral code, no God, would do far worse. I wanted to cry out, "No! You're wrong! You're doing the devil's work!" I wanted to sound like Singer and rally the zombies to rebellion, but I just stood and trembled. Children, children, children? Even you can't justify this! Or was he right? God only knew.

Fearful wailing arose all around. Angry cries mixed in with the tears. And everywhere armed guards were poised. I saw them on their perches, rifles loaded, machine guns aimed, so nobody rebelled, nobody rose against them…against him. God was silent as always.

He wants our children? I still wasn't crying. Why not? Had all these months of being the receptacle of intolerable news and tragic rumors hardened me to the truly intolerable? I still couldn't believe it was happening, here, to us, essential to the German empire. Did I think we were immune? Yes, we were protected. The Chairman will not let anything happen to the children of his friends, the inner circle, the administrators of this hellish circus. That is why I wasn't afraid. He was addressing the masses, the new immigrants, the lazy unemployed, not his chosen officials, his loyal supporters, those who were his true believers. We kept the machine running. Without us, there would be no ghetto. The German Empire depends on us. It was a lie, but I had to believe it. Wasn't that why the Gestapo wasn't mowing us down with their machine guns as we trembled, cowards, in the square?

The Chairman gripped the microphone again, his voice quivering. "I have not come today to console you. Nor have I come today to calm you, but to uncover all your sorrow and pain. I have come like a robber to take away from you the best from under your hearts! I tried with all my abilities to get the decree revoked."

This caught the attention of the crowd. Hope. Hands were clenched in prayer.

The Chairman continued, "After trying to get it revoked was impossible, I attempted to moderate it. Just yesterday, I arranged a registration of all nine-year-old children. I wanted to rescue at least that single year, from nine to ten years old."

The expectancy was palpable, people craning their necks to catch the next hopeful words. If he could register nine-year-olds for work, at least they would be saved. It had always worked before.

Rumkowski shook his head. "But they did not want to grant this to me. One thing I succeeded at—to save the children from ten years and up. Let this be our comfort in our great sorrow."

I caught a few breathing a sigh of relief, but the weeping was an undercurrent that rose and swelled like ocean tides.

The Chairman sounded paternal. "We have in the ghetto many sick with tuberculosis whose lives are counted in days, maybe really in weeks. I don't know. Maybe it's a devilish plan, maybe not. I cannot refrain from pronouncing it: "Give me these sick, and in their place, healthy people can be saved." I know how everyone cherishes a patient in his home, all the more so among Jews. But at every decree, we must weigh and measure: Who should, can, and may be saved?"

Now each of us was to play God? We were to choose who was too sick to live? Cukier? His name appeared before me as if lit by lightning. Is that what had happened to him? Did he volunteer to save the life of a healthy man, woman, or child? Did his landlady turn him in to spare someone else? My God, he's gone! Julian! It struck hard that I would never see my friend again. Rosenfeld had vanished...Cukier, dear Julian. I clutched the bowl of the pipe in my pocket.

The Chairman kept speaking: "Common sense requires that saved must be that which can be saved and has prospects of surviving, and not that which cannot be saved anyway."

Two plus two equals four. Of course, Rumkowski's solution makes sense, but then why does it hurt so much? Why is it so unacceptable? I shivered. Julian would never return to our room. All his brave and agonized efforts to support our Leader had not saved him. Rumkowski was presenting logic to people who couldn't accept the inevitability. I couldn't accept it. It was immoral. It was wrong. But Regina was safe. She was an administrator's protected child. I had to hear more. What else could he say to justify his obscene demands?

"We are living in the ghetto. Our life is so austere that we don't have enough for the healthy, much less for the sick. Each of us feeds the sick person at the expense of his own health. We give our bread away to the sick person. We give him our bit of sugar, our piece of meat and the result is not only that the patient becomes no healthier from it, but also we become sick."

Yes, very logical again, but I saw Miriam sneering. She and Singer, even Heilig, and myself now, would never believe logic overrides conscience. Did Rumkowski really think we believed this nonsensical appeal for sacrifice when he chain-smoked real cigarettes while we starved? Hunger was everywhere. It had unleashed battles for crumbs of bread, but could we sacrifice our own brothers and sisters, so we might have a little extra at our meals? Had we become cannibals? One look around, and I could not be sure. Emaciated bodies, barely enough flesh and muscle to stand, weaved precariously with his words. We were a horde of boneless, starving, zombies, so lost that we could accept this tragedy as inevitable.

Rumkowski sounded as if he understood our pain: "Of course, such victims are the handsomest and the most noble. But in a time when we must choose: to sacrifice the sick person who not only has the least chance of recovery but is also likely to make others sick; or to save a healthy person—I could not delve long into the problem and had to decide it for the good of the healthy one. I have therefore in that sense instructed the physicians, and they will be compelled to turn in all incurable patients in order to be able to rescue in their place healthy people who want and are able to live on..."

The outcry was immediate and terrible. "You bastard! Would you sacrifice your brother, your sister, who is ill, so a stranger can live?" Another cried, "You are the devil. Lies! All lies!"

My eyes rushed to the Germans. They weren't moving. Were there smiles on the Gestapo's faces? Did I hear the click of their weapons unlocking? Machine gun belts readied?

I wished the Chairman would end this most horrible of speeches, but he persisted. Why? Didn't he understand his pleas were useless? He'd failed us. He was sacrificing our children so he and his family could thrive under the Nazi patronage he'd cultivated at our expense. That's what Miriam and Singer argued all along. I still wasn't sure what I believed. I was afraid that I was insane. Nothing was real.

Rumkowski stared down at us through his eyeglasses, his voice exuding compassion. "I understand you, mothers. I see your tears quite well. I also feel your hearts, fathers, that tomorrow, immediately after your child will have been taken away from you, you will have to go to work, while just yesterday you still played with your dear kids."

It was finally penetrating my brain. The devil really wanted their children. I held Regina on the floor yesterday...he wasn't talking about me. Regina was protected. Rumkowski needed us, would protect us. Why was I even here? I wanted to leave but couldn't. This was a fatal car crash, the victims all around me, bloodied and broken. I hated the horror, the gore, but I couldn't look away. I couldn't walk away. I am a reporter. I must bear witness to the tragedy the others must suffer. The speech is too long. End their suffering?

The Chairman's thick mane of white hair made him look like God with the sky and clouds as his backdrop. We were all familiar with his imperial visage. His crown of white hair dominated in large photographs. His face, stern, authoritarian, was posted in every factory, in every warehouse, in every school. He was our father, our savior, our God, and now he was crying in front of us, asking for our pity?

Rumkowski's voice thundered again, "I know all of this and I feel it. Since 4 o'clock yesterday, since I found out about the decree, I am entirely broken down. I am living with your grief and your pain torments me and I don't know how and with what strength I will be able to survive it." He leaned closer and lowered his voice as if confiding to a close friend. "I must disclose to you a secret: 24,000 victims were demanded. Through eight days of three thousand people each day, but I succeeded in pushing the number down to twenty thousand, even less than 20,000, but on condition that there will be children up to ten years old. Children from eleven years and up are secure. Since the children together with the elderly give only a number of approximately 13,000 souls, it will be necessary to fill the gap with sick people too."

Now who is playing the number game, I thought, as people all around me focused on the Chairman's shuffling of their friends, families and coworkers, all to appease the insatiable German appetite for Jewish souls…Jewish children, useless to their war effort. Children, mouths to feed, in the Nazi equation, useless at labor. Useless? Did the Nazis not have children? Could they not identify with our pain? Were they truly without souls and hearts? How could they want our children? Thousands of children? They will change their mind when they stare into the children's faces. Regina's eyes melt stone.

Zombies were weeping pitifully, swaying on bodies weakened by hunger, and now this new grief. I was terrified of them, afraid they would stir their meatless bones and riot. The Gestapo would respond. Their machine guns were ready. I could hear their explosive blasts in my tortured brain. Oh God, end this speech? God, please?

The Chairman held up his hands for silence.

The guards eyed the crowd.

Did the Jewish police have children? Had their emotions become extinct? Were their children protected too? Was compassion just another corpse in the ghetto?

The Chairman did sound compassionate: "It is difficult for me to speak. I don't have any strength. I only want to say to you my request: Help me carry out the action! I am trembling. I fear that others will, God forbid, take over the implementation into their hands...A broken Jew is standing before you. Don't envy me. It is the most difficult decree that I have ever had to carry out. I extend to you, my broken, trembling arms and I beg: Give the victims into my hands, in order through them to avoid additional victims, in order to protect a congregation of a hundred thousand Jews. They promised me so: If we ourselves deliver our victims, there will be calm..."

A cry arose from somewhere in the crowd. "We'll all go! We'll all go!" It became a chant. Someone shouted: "No family should lose their only child ... take children from those who have others!" Suddenly, voices were shouting out ideas, anything to avoid losing all of the children, all the precious treasures we could not believe would have to be sacrificed. Each person was convinced they had the answer that could end this nightmare.

The Chairman again silenced the mob, his hands outstretched like Moses. "These are empty phrases! I don't have any strength to conduct discussions with you! If someone will come from the authorities, no one will yell..."

I understood what he meant. But was he right? He was shouting at us that if the Germans were the ones demanding this outrage, nobody would dare protest. Nobody would even whisper their thoughts questioning the wolves' demands, not with their weapons aimed into our faces. Did he really believe that? As I stared around me at the mob, I wondered if the authorities were on the stage and not the beleaguered Chairman, if a few brave souls in the crowd would have dared the guns to save their children. Warsaw had risen up against the Nazis. Warsaw was no more. We were starving, beaten dogs, unable to fight even to save our sweetest gifts from God.

For a second, I thought Rumkowski was going to walk away, but he summoned what little strength he claimed to possess and spoke again. "I understand what it means to tear off a limb from the body. Yesterday, I pleaded on my knees, but it was no use. From small towns that possessed 7,000 to 8,000 Jews barely 1,000 have arrived here. What then is better? What are you asking for? To leave 80,000 to 90,000 Jews alive or, God forbid, to annihilate everybody?"

He had finally spoken of the unspeakable: "annihilate." At last, it was out in the open. No more lies and promises, no more false hope. The Chairman, the Eldest of the Jews, was now a defrocked Wizard of Oz with one last trick to save a desperate community facing annihilation.

The thunder was gone. The man who had been king was now a subject like the rest of us. "Judge as you wish: my obligation is to take care of the remnant of Jews. I am not talking to hotheads—I will continue to do everything to prevent weapons being brought into the streets and blood being shed. The decree did not permit us to get it revoked; it only allowed itself to be reduced. One needs the heart of a bandit in order to ask for what I am asking of you. But put yourself in my position, think logically, and you yourself will come to the conclusion that you cannot act differently because the number of the portion that can be saved is much larger than the part that must be surrendered."

Totally logical, but logic wasn't working. I felt pity for the weeping zombies. I started to walk, parting them as I tried to separate myself from those who had to suffer. I felt for them, felt pain throughout my body and soul. But what could anyone do if the great Eldest of the Jews was powerless? His voice was no longer blasting from the stage. I looked up.

The Chairman had replaced his hat. The terrible oration was over. Message delivered. Fronted by his guards, he made his way from the stage. He leaned on Neftalin's shoulder as he climbed into his coach. The "clip-clop" of his horse, slow and loud on the cobblestones, was soon followed by the sound of a German staff car, and then trucks filled with soldiers.

The crowd remained, stunned, shocked, seeking comfort from each other. Some rushed to leave, to save their children, but most remained, unable to believe what they'd heard. The Chairman's speech completed the transformation. I was surrounded by zombies.

I rushed through the mob, anticipating the police eventually acting to disperse the mourners, the defiant, the ones teetering, fainting onto the muddy ground. I had to get back to our office. I had to write my report. While it was fresh in my mind, I had to write my report…

CHAPTER 44

By the time I got to our room, the horror of what I'd witnessed finally sank in. "Were you there for the Chairman's speech?" I asked, falling into a chair, contemplating how I would record this event.

"I'm writing it up now. I feel terrible for anyone with children," Zelkowicz said.

Regina is safe, I repeated in my mind. I tried to capture my thoughts to objectively describe Rumkowski's arguments. I couldn't focus. I felt as if I was choking, the room more stifling than ever. Inexplicably, tears welled up in my eyes.

"Do you want me to read my analysis aloud?" Jozef asked.

"It must be included, preserved for the future." I thought of all the other countless pages we'd compiled and all the men who had spent their final days in this room: Rosenfeld, Singer, Cukier...all gone. Where? God and the Germans know. My brain screamed this is futile, useless, a waste. You should be fighting, fighting anyway you can. I am fighting, the only way I think will make a difference. "Yes, read it."

Zelkowicz straightened the paper. "Even now it is difficult to grasp what has occurred. An elemental force has passed through the ghetto and swept away some 15,000 people." He looked at me. "No one knows the exact number yet..."

Numbers...numbers...numbers...all reduced to numerals. I listened but did not listen. I was here, but I was not.

Jozef's voice droned on.

I was barely able to focus. It was only back here, in our conference room, our sanctum, listening to Jozef's account of what he had experienced, that the full impact hit me. The devil wants all our children. Regina? "I must go," I said.

Zelkowicz looked startled.

"I have a child," I said, but it sounded as if someone was speaking from a distance.

"You have a child? Yes, go."

I should have waited for Heilig, a last effort to force his help, but there was no time. Had Miriam already heard of the speech?

I was about to leave the building. One hope. I crossed the hall to Neftalin's office. He would provide the answer I needed. While I was confident Regina was safe, hearing it from him, the Deputy, my friend, would erase all doubt. Surely, a few children would be spared to keep our people from extinction. Rumkowski's children were protected. The devil promised.

Neftalin's office was vacant.

I asked Dora Fuchs, the Chairman's secretary and learned that Neftalin, the Commandant of the Order Service and members of the Resettlement Commission had been ordered to 4 Koscielny Square.

I walked as quickly as I could, forcing myself not to run. I waved my pass to a guard and was allowed inside the dark entryway. In the hall, another guard directed me to the fourth floor. On the third landing, I fell against the wall, unable to breathe. Regina's face appeared in the shadows cast by the naked bulb hanging from the ceiling. "I have to go," I rasped to the shadowy hands stretching toward me.

On the fourth floor, I waved my pass and asked for Deputy Neftalin.

"I don't know him," the guard replied.

"He's Deputy to the Chairman. He's here," I said.

"He might be with the others. A bunch of official looking people just arrived." He leaned toward me. "Any idea what's going on?"

I shook my head.

He nodded. "Try over there. If you learn anything..."

I was already walking.

Another guard admitted me to a large room filled with rectangular tables. A corps of men and women were standing around piles of cards. I walked toward the closest table. They were feverishly writing on the cards.

"What are you doing?" I asked a young woman.

She glanced up. I saw Miriam's distrusting eyes.

I showed my I.D., hoping my hands weren't trembling.

"We have to copy the names and ages of every ghetto resident."

"That's a huge job," I said.

The woman nodded. "More than 150,000." She frowned. "It's around the clock. We have forty people changing every eight hours."

Numbers? Is this what I sound like to others? "What are they doing all this for?"

She gave me an impatient look. "Nothing is being left to chance. The lists will be arranged by street and then sent to individual Order Service precincts for execution. Now, please, allow me to complete my work?"

How could she be so unemotional? Hadn't she heard the Chairman's speech? Didn't she understand this was devil's work? "Thank you."

She didn't reply. Her pencil was marking up a card.

I started away but stopped, gazed at her again. In appearance, she reminded me of a younger Miriam, but there was none of my wife's warmth. She's a zombie condemning other zombies, I was eager to get out of the room with all the robotic pens creating a book of the dead.

"I must see Deputy Neftalin," I demanded of a guard blocking the office door.

"Nobody gets in," He said, both hands gripping his club.

I showed him my pass. "Deputy Neftalin is a personal friend."

"Our orders are nobody gets in. Now get to work before I report you."

"Please, sir, I have a one-year-old daughter?" Was this really me? I was begging.

The officer glanced around and then whispered, "We have our orders from the Chairman. You must leave now. If someone sees you, your daughter will be in danger of losing her father. Please go?" He straightened up and became an unseeing sentry again.

Chilled by his threat, I thought of storming past him, but that wasn't me. I wanted to beg again but sensed it was hopeless. Orders are orders. Heilig! We must act now, I thought, racing back to the Jewish ghetto administration building. There was no more time.

When I entered our room, Heilig stared at me with fearful eyes. "I know what you want. I heard the speech too. You should know people have died. My friends have died. There is no escape. I'm truly sorry—"

"You promised. You damn well promised!" I pulled him out of his chair by his shirt collar.

He pulled away. The shirt was so old. I had a piece of his collar in my hand. He screeched at me, "Singer is dead! He was killed in Warsaw! There is nothing I can do for you! Nothing! We are in the same boat! You are no better than anyone else here!"

I held my fist shaking in his face. "You bastard! I won't lose my Regina!" I threw myself at him, punching him hard in the stomach. "You promised. Now, look! Now, look what you've done to me!" I was wild, punching him again and again. All my frustrations and anger were in my fists. I'd never hurt anyone before, but I struck again and again.

Heilig doubled over, blood spitting from his mouth. He was crying. "I tried. I tried. What more do you want? I tried. Kill me! Kill me! It doesn't matter. We're all dead."

I stopped hitting him, staring at the blood dripping from his face, tears falling to the floor. "You little cowardly shit."

He was blubbering, doubled over, hands clutching his stomach. "Singer wanted to help you. He offered months ago. You were too good. He wanted to take you to the black market. You would have made connections. No. You wanted him to do your dirty work. You're the coward. He wanted to save her—"

"Shut up, you, weasel." I was ready to go at him again, but what good would it do? I was trembling with rage and frustration.

Heilig cowered in the corner. "I tried to find a way. I tried. You know I tried."

I glanced at him. Maybe he was telling the truth? Maybe he had tried? I glared at my fists. What was happening to me? I unclenched my hands. "I'm sorry. I'm sorry." I walked toward him, extending my hand to help him get up.

He pulled closer to the wall. "You never liked me. You just wanted to use me. Keep away."

I withdrew my hand. Heilig was right I never did like him. The Weasel I called him. I had to think. "Singer is dead? You know this for a fact?"

"He was in Warsaw."

"Is he dead? Are you sure?" How could I tell Miriam? Tears were in my eyes, but not in front of this sonofabitch.

"A newcomer told me." He was wiping the blood with his sleeve.

"Fighting the Germans?"

"That's why he left here."

I thought of Singer's note. I knew it wasn't the only reason he left. A sense of hopelessness slammed down on me. "There's no escape, is there?"

"I'm sorry. I tried." Heilig was sniveling into his bloody hand. "Don't you think I would have left if I could?"

"Can we bribe someone…a sentry?"

"We tried. The Gestapo has tightened the noose. We've lost many trying to escape." He pulled himself up. "You are the keeper of the death records. Some of those shot and tortured…they were my friends. They were working to find ways to get you out." He wiped his nose with his filthy sleeve again. "You must believe me, we are still trying, but nothing is getting in or out anymore." He looked at me with tears in his eyes. "I'm trapped too."

I sank into my chair. "Clean yourself up." I threw my handkerchief at the floor. "I don't know what came over me. It won't happen again. I'm sorry."

He remained leaning against the wall, his voice muffled. "Your daughter is beautiful. I feel for you. Oscar loved your family. He asked me to watch over them...you. I would feel how you feel if I had someone like your little girl." He returned to his seat, eyes on me as if fearing I'd attack again. "I said things—"

"It's okay." I wiped the tears from my face with my sleeve. "I know you tried. I should have listened to Oscar long ago. It's not your fault." I rose from my chair, thought of extending my hand again, to beg him to forget what a fool I'd been to attack him, but I didn't deserve his forgiveness. I didn't deserve Singer's forgiveness either. How could I tell Miriam about him? Miriam would never forgive me if we lost Regina. "Maybe the Chairman will change the Germans' minds? He says he's still trying to work on them. Maybe they'll change their minds?"

"We can pray for that."

Yes, we can pray for that, I thought.

"I'm not giving up," Heilig said, as I walked from the room. "I promise you."

I straightened up passing the guards. The Gestapo had replaced the Chairman's force in the building and square. I could almost feel their hatred burning through the large yellow star sewn to the back of my coat.

By now Miriam would know. What would I face when I told her there was nothing we could do?

The streets were deserted. The Chairman had issued a proclamation that all inhabitants were banned from being outdoors after 5 p.m. I had to hurry home. The Jewish police and Kripo were everywhere. If they didn't enforce the curfew, the Nazis would. I walked fast, afraid to run, afraid of being arrested, afraid of not getting home in time to protect Regina. I raised my eyes to the sky. If only I saw airplanes? If only God would finally open his eyes and show mercy? "God, let the bombs fall? Let the bombs fall?"

CHAPTER 45

SEPTEMBER 5, 1942
Pedestrian traffic after 5 p.m. has been suspended until further notice.

When I pushed open the door, Miriam was on the floor, clutching Regina so tightly to her body that the child looked frightened.

I had rehearsed so many things I wanted to say, but Miriam was rocking back and forth, some unintelligible melody coming from her lips which were hidden in Regina's hair. I stole closer, but it was as if Miriam didn't see me. She was singing a lullaby to the child she knew she must lose.

I sat down on the chair in the room lit by one candle and could do nothing but wait. My mind was searching for some answer. There had to be something I could do. Heilig, Singer, someone would come for them. It wasn't too late. It couldn't be.

In time, the silence calmed me. Miriam's rocking of Regina, the endless almost inaudible song, repeated and repeated, was lulling me as well. I thought of Miriam when I first saw her. She was so young and fresh-looking, her body soft, still with baby-fat on her cheeks. I found it hard to believe her parents were giving her to me. Her father said, "You are a good man. Take care of her always." I tried. I thought back to the first time I held Regina. Her little heart was tapping away against my bare chest. I tickled her tiny, pink, foot and marveled at the perfect little toes. I felt her delicate fingers wrap around my thumb...I heard her breathing.

There was the sound of footsteps on our stairs. Voices erupted. Someone was screaming in the flats below us. An explosion? A gunshot startled me to our reality. I leaped from my chair. "Give her to me," I screamed at Miriam, but she held tight. "Give her to me!" I seized Regina from Miriam's hands. "We'll hide her." I held Regina close to me and rushed toward the small closet. "You must be quiet," I said. "You must stay here. We'll play our game. You hide." I placed her in the back of the dark closet. "You are so smart…so good. I'll cover you." I dropped a tattered blanket over her and topped it with a thin layer of our soiled laundry. "Don't move. Don't say anything. It's our game. Remember, sweetheart, you must be quiet to win." I kissed her cheek. "Papa loves you. Stay still now. Remember our game."

Miriam moved to get into the closet.

"No. She's safe. We must be ready. They're coming."

Miriam looked dully at me as if she didn't understand.

"She will be okay. We've played this game many times before." I bent over Regina. "Go to sleep now. Don't make a sound. Remember our little game."

I heard voices shouting in German, "Out! Everyone out!"

"It will be alright. We've played this game before…many times." I grabbed Miriam's hand and led her away. I closed the closet. "Be good, Regina. Hide from daddy." The bellowing and crashing footsteps were louder. I thought of remaining inside. I held my official identification card in my hand. It would save us. It would protect Regina. "Come, Miriam, we must go out." I pulled her toward me and kissed her forehead. "I love you."

"Regina," she whispered.

"She'll be fine. She knows the game." Oh God, I thought, please don't let her be frightened? I pulled Miriam with me. She tried to break away. "No. You must not fight me."

"Out! Get out, everyone!" The German voices were accompanied by the sound of rickety doors being smashed in by rifle butts and battering rams. The men on the stairs, their boots pounding the bare wood stairs, were Gestapo. Where were the Jewish police? "Get out, you filthy Jews! All of you on the street! Get out!"

I held up my I.D. to one of the black shadows. "Get out! I'll smash your face," he screamed and shoved me down the step.

I almost fell, but held my balance, still grasping Miriam's hand.

More demons raced up the stairs, smashing rifle butts against doors, hurling everyone out of the apartments if they dared to hide. The screaming and crying were terrible.

I glanced at our door. It was still closed.

"Get out! Get out! You filthy dogs!" A rough hand shoved me through the door and almost threw me down the front steps to the street. "Miriam!" I held on as she struggled to break away. There were people everywhere. They were shivering in the night, standing in crooked lines, every resident on the block. Black-circled eyes stared in fear at the surreal landscape of our buildings being ravaged by the uniformed German invaders.

'Miriam, no!" She was still trying to pull free.

People were in pajamas. Didn't they know what was happening? Maybe they didn't believe it? Who could? I was still clutching my Identification card.

A large truck grabbed my attention. The back was open. Parents were holding their children tightly against their bodies. More trucks arrived, backs open like hungry mouths.

A German officer was staring impassively at us.

I avoided his eyes. He was studying us as if we were insects not worthy of compassion. I had to try. I held my identification card in front of me and took a few steps forward, Miriam a few steps behind. I held my card higher.

An armed guard stepped quickly between us and using his rifle shoved me back. "Step away, Jewish pig," he rasped. I saw his eyes land on Miriam and pulled her behind me. I felt as if his eyes were saying, "How does dog like you deserve such a woman?"

It seemed like hours that we were kept waiting. The Germans were going through every apartment, every nook and cranny, while we, broken and beaten by all we had suffered, remained in our hopeless dim-witted bodies, on a line where all we had in common was our shared terror.

And then the horror began. I tried not to see, not to hear. Screams rose like flames all around me as German hands pried the children away from their parents' bodies. The sound of rifle butts smashing into faces and stomachs, grown men crying as they fell to the ground, their sons and daughters torn away from them...and the sight of German soldiers throwing children into the trucks. I closed my eyes, praying...praying...God, why don't you hear us? Why do you not see us?

The screams and wails filled my ears. I looked at Miriam, and her eyes were wide with fear. "It will be alright," I whispered, but how could she hear me in the terrible storm of wailing all around us.

I looked at the truck. A mother was reaching up for her child.

A German soldier sneered at her. "You want to join him?" He smashed her stomach with his rifle butt. "Get away, Jewish bitch." He laughed and threw her back to the ground. When her husband reached for her, the rifle broke his jaw and sent blood down his face.

I'd never seen anything like this. I was not prepared for the brutality of the German policemen. Rage filled me, but there was nothing anyone could do. The black-uniformed troops were armed with rifles. A few machine guns were stationed at various points along the street. We could have mounted an attack, but they would have mowed us down. We were like sheep. Singer said that. "Where are the Davids, the Maccabees, the Bar Kochbas, the heroes of yesterday?" He had asked, and I replied, "The war will be over soon." And now, he, the brave hero, was reportedly dead, and I, the sheep, was shivering with fear in the cold night. They were taking our children. There was no fight left in us. We could barely breathe...barely stand.

The trucks were nearly full. Children were screaming, some bloodied and reaching for parents no longer in sight. Parents were in agony, unable to do anything against the barricade of armed Gestapo.

I covered my ears. Nothing sealed out the sounds.

The commander said something to one of his officers and the soldiers descended upon us again. This time their hands gruffly seized anyone who they deemed sickly or elderly. Hands tried to keep onto their aged and sick relatives, but rifles swung cruelly, and the screams echoed in my head. "Stand straight, Miriam," I ordered, "Look good." I yanked her up, forced her to stand erect. "Pay attention. Regina is safe."

At Regina's name, she straightened up, more aware. She looked around us, and her lips stopped quivering.

The soldiers barely glanced at me. But some paused, struck by Miriam's eyes. Even now, after everything we'd been through, her eyes were haunting.

I glanced at the trucks. Old men and women were holding the children on the open truck backs. The young ones, none over ten years of age, although some older were taken since nobody looked at papers, were crying and screaming for their parents, who were weeping helplessly. Who could believe such a nightmare?

A truck motor roared to life. It woke us again to what was happening. They were leaving. The beast had filled its stomach. Regina was safe. In seconds, it would be over. Too many were in the belly of the monsters. We were still here.

And then I saw a tiny pair of eyes searching the crowd from over the shoulder of a young policeman, whose face appeared too handsomely etched for his demonic role.

Oh God, no! I pushed ahead for a better view. "Regina!" I screamed, not believing my eyes, not feeling fear, only a mindless need to charge through the line and grab my tiny, squirming child from the beastly black-gloved hands. I shoved aside a zombie moaning in front of me; a woman, blood dripping down her face; other zombies. I pushed through them as if they didn't exist. "Regina!"

"Get back Jewish dog!"

I held my identification in my shaking hand. "Mine kind. My child," I said in German, "Please? Please? She's only a baby?"

A rifle butt slammed into my stomach. I screamed in agony and keeled forward. "Mine kind. My child. Mine liebchen." I gasped, tears breaking from the pain.

"Jewish bastard, you want more?" The butt raised to my face.

The pain in my gut, the shock, was excruciating. My hands over my face, I slinked away, a worm crawling in the dirt.

The soldier spat at my legs. "Coward."

"I tried," I whined, unable to rise. "Forgive me?" I reached for Miriam's hand.

Fear shot through me. She wasn't here. "Where is she?" From the ground, I saw the back of her legs, those beautiful legs. She was advancing to the front of the line. "Oh, God! No more." I snaked through crowded mourners, crying, wailing, clutching each other. "Miriam! For God's sake, Miriam!" I saw her. She was ahead, slicing her way through the crowd. I tried to stand. The pain where the rifle had struck hurt like nothing I'd ever felt, but I scrambled toward her, bent over, my hand clutching my stomach. A hunchback, I stumbled, pushed away anyone in my path, not caring about their pain or if I knocked them to the ground. I had to stop her. What was she doing? "I love you," I screamed. "Miriam, come back! Miriam?"

Miriam was near the head of the line.

"What are you doing?"

The trucks were only yards ahead.

"Miriam! Please?" I was almost there. I saw her face. "Please, see me? Stop!"

Miriam turned.

"Forgive me?" I cried, scrambling toward her.

She straightened her hair and her dress.

I was almost there.

Miriam pushed through the line of zombies, their eyes raised to the trucks. Men stared helplessly, cowering in the muck...like I was...but

Miriam was standing.

I couldn't get up. God, I wanted to. The pain. I wormed toward her. "I can't lose you," I screamed. "God, no more. No dammit more!" My mind was unable to take this agony. "Miriam. Please?"

Miriam strode past the line across from a Gestapo officer. He had a stick poised to strike her.

I was almost caught up. "Miriam! No. Come back?"

A rifle butt slammed into my face. My scream was inhuman, bestial. I fell to the ground. I was writhing on the floor, tears blinding me…too far to reach her. Blood was on my hands. Blood flowed from my jaw. I had to stop her. In the muck, I tried to pull my body forward. "Oh, God."

Miriam was standing in front of the officer, her hazel eyes staring into the German officer's face. Her lips were moving. What was she saying? I was too far away to hear. "You can't talk to them. They're animals."

I saw soldiers, weapons raised on either side of her. One was aimed at her. Was his finger on the trigger? I waited for the bark of the rifle, praying…praying…face barely held out of the muck. Her face. I did not want to see what his bullet could do to that beautiful face. "Please God? I'm begging you." I rose to my knees, my hand on my broken jaw, my eyes on the rifle.

"Get back you filthy Jew!" A soldier shoved me to the ground and held the barrel of his rifle in my stomach, his eyes watching the drama of Miriam and his commanding officer.

"Meine frau…my wife."

"Is that your woman?" He asked with a cruel sneer. "You don't deserve her." He raised the barrel to my face. "You Jews are all cowards."

I should have attacked him. I should have let him kill me, but all I could think about in my broken mind was that Regina, my angel, was still hiding in the closet. She needed me. Play the game, sweetheart. You'll be safe. Play the game. She was safe. It was some other child the soldier had been holding when he exited our tenement. I couldn't bear the truth. It was all a nightmare. I'll wake up. Regina, my brilliant child, will be in the closet, waiting for me to find her. "It's hide-and-seek, my little one. Daddy is coming."

Miriam's back was toward me. Did she smile at the officer? I didn't know, but I imagined. "Please, don't hurt her? Miriam?"

The officer said something to his guard who stepped aside and let her by.

Miriam walked toward the trucks.

Soldiers near the vehicles aimed their rifles.

The officer Miriam had been with shouted an order to the guards. They lowered the rifles that had been riveted on her and watched silently as Miriam approached. She stopped walking. "Thank God," I said, thinking she was coming back.

Miriam searched the crowd. Were her eyes looking for me? She began to walk again.

I wanted to wave, to shout, "I'm here! I'm here!" A rifle was inches from my face. I tasted blood in my mouth. Regina was safe, hiding in our closet. I could not let her lose both of us. "Oh God, help me?" Tears flowed down my cracked face…acid burning my flesh. I wanted to stand but could only watch from the dirt.

Miriam reached the truck. She stood behind it searching the open back.

"Regina needs you," I cried when I saw her smile back at me.

The guards aimed their rifles.

They're going to shoot her, my brain screamed.

The commanding officer shouted to the guards, "Let her go if that is her wish."

One of the guards lowered his weapon. He held up his hideous black glove.

Miriam climbed up without his assistance.

I tried to stand again, but the pain was terrible. The rifle barrel was a guard dog in my face. I saw the truck through a veil of blood.

The dragon roars of the trucks were met by a wave of crying.

The guards tensed, rifles, machine guns, ready for any movement that appeared a threat. Jews disappeared every day, and nobody cared how.

No need to fear us. It was as if we were already dead.

The last sight I had of Miriam, she was standing in the back of the truck with a small girl clutched to her heart. I should have known she would not let the children go off on their own. My sweet wife, like our great Chairman, loved children.

The trucks were swallowed by the night.

"You, cowardly Jewish shit," the Nazi hissed and lowered his rifle. "Your wife is more of a man than you."

"Regina needs me," I replied, a bloody mess on the wet ground, wondering why everyone was crying. It was a beautiful night... diamond stars in the cold sky. The blackout made them seem so close. So blindingly close.

I heard strange sounds. The undercurrent of sobs and praying was low and persistent, real, yet unreal.

The soldiers left.

I looked around. People were in the street, crying, wringing their hands. Couples, no longer able to shed tears, began to leave. Some held each other up, crippled by their loss. Some blamed each other and walked away from their shell-shocked partners. Many cursed Rumkowski's name. Some blessed him. They had no children, or their children were older...or they were just grateful to have escaped one more deportation to the unknown. "The devil you know..."

I don't know how long I remained outside. It began to rain. The drops were cold. Miriam will wonder what happened to me? Regina needs me to find her. I imagined her giggles when I would dig her out from her hiding place. I pulled myself to my knees. My stomach and jaw still hurt like hell. I smelled blood, tasted it inside my mouth. It didn't matter. It was over. The pogrom was over. No more wolves...not tonight.

I dragged my wet body up the steps. I heard a few muffled moans coming from behind doors, most no longer able to close, smashed in by rifle butts…a scattering of bullet holes. I smelled smoke, or was it gunpowder?

I reached our flat on the top floor, cursing again those who stole our banister for heat. As Rosenfeld always says, "Desperate people do desperate things." Wait until I tell the old man and Cukier about our close call tonight." Tears burned my eyes. I looked down at the bottom of the stairs and almost lost my balance. I fought a strange longing to leap over the railing and fly, to soar down to the hard concrete below. But Regina needed me.

"Miriam, I'm home," I called softly, to not awaken Regina. "I wonder where she is?" I was used to seeing Miriam playing with Regina on the floor. "Miri? Regina? I'm home." And then I remembered the closet, our little game of hide-and-seek…the game we had played so many times. "You hide, little Regina, my sweet. Be nice and quiet. I'll come and get you later…later." I remembered kissing her on the forehead and covering her with the blanket. "She's such a good girl. Even now, she is silent, waiting for her Papa. I'm coming, my angel."

Why is the closet open? I always close it after I hide her.

At first, it was too dark to see, but there she was, still wrapped in her tiny blanket. "What a good girl." I picked up the blanket and held it in my arms, clutching it against my chest. Carrying it gently so she would not wake, I returned to my chair. Her heart was beating against my heart, the most wonderful feeling a parent could have. Suddenly, I remembered the other parents, their children torn away. How sad. How tragic. I pulled Regina even closer, grateful I could hold her when other parents could not hold their children anymore. That was the reward of being in Rumkowski's inner circle. "Tomorrow, I'll write about those poor souls and their lost children. Miriam will return soon. The war will be over any day now. America is in the battle, and Russia, as it did to Napoleon, is turning our uniforms red. It will be alright, dear Regina. Now sleep. I'll protect you…always."

In the dark, my eyes were riveted on the door. I remembered rumors about the Nazis bashing in doors and sending Jews far away. "That will never happen in Lodz. We were safe here." Tears streamed down my face. "Miriam?" I clutched my baby closer. "Mommy will be home soon."

An eternity later, I fell asleep. The empty tear-stained blanket fell to the floor.

THE END

WHAT HAPPENED TO THE LODZ GHETTO?

A t this point, Book 2 ends, but it would be wrong of me to leave you completely in the dark about what happened to the actual inhabitants of the Lodz ghetto, and to their controversial leader. I will conclude this story of love, friendship and courage in Book 3, but until that time, please visit my website at www.newhousecreativegroup.com to learn more about the fate of Rumkowski and the ghetto. Better yet, read the actual *Chronicle of the Lodz Ghetto,* edited by Lucjan Dobroszycki, (Yale University Press,1984). I've never read a more chilling account of what the occupied Jews suffered than these anonymous entries that build to a tragic conclusion. My novel is fiction based on what are, unfortunately, documented events. I lost my grandparents and most of my relatives in the ghetto and concentration camps and still don't know their exact fate. There are no tombstones. The Holocaust is the shadow that has haunted me all my life.

SUNDAY, JULY 30, 1944 is the final known Chronicle entry: population was 68,561. The following is the entire entry: *...the crucial question remains: What is there to eat?*

Among the less than 5,000 survivors of the Lodz ghetto were a young woman and man destined to become my parents. How did they survive? They never said, and I was too frightened to ask. I knew almost nothing about their ordeal until I read the **Chronicle**. I hope my novel honors them, and all the victims and survivors. Only knowledge can prevent history from repeating. Thank you for sharing this experience with me. Please invite your friends and family to read my book, so we may all say, "Never again to anyone."

NOTE: About the *Chronicle of the Lodz Ghetto*

My historical fiction series follows the timeline of events detailed in *The Chronicle of the Lodz Ghetto*, translated and edited by Lucjan Dobroszycki, (Yale University Press, 1984). While the names of some characters are real, any resemblance to actual persons are fictitious, unintended, and should not be inferred. The exception is Chairman Rumkowski whose policies and actions are still hotly debated. I'm not a good enough writer to create such a controversial figure.

While this work is fiction based on real events, I've attempted to retain the tone and style of the original entries as they appear in the Chronicle, including grammatical errors and irregularities: e.g., the inconsistent titles of the entries. I decided to include these excerpts and titles because on their own they present a grim outline of the steps leading to the ghetto's fall. I selected those that best fit my dramatization and made the decision to retain their authentic character. I didn't want to 'touch one hair' fearing to dilute the 'chill' factor I experienced in reading them. The Chronicle is an amazing document that miraculously survived when the only surviving author, no spoilers, recovered copies of the pages that had been hidden from the Nazis. But that's a story for Book 3.

The **Chronicle** raises many troubling questions. When did the ghetto residents know the fate of the deportees? Why did the entries lack emotion? Who wrote the individual accounts? What did the Chroniclers really think of their leader? What would we have done in his shoes? Finally, was he a saint or the Devil? As Rumkowski said, "Someday, I will be judged." Book 3: *The Noose Closes*, will provide more clues. I leave it to the reader to decide.

For my parents and my relatives who died in Lodz and the death camps; for the victims and survivors of hate and genocide, past, present and future.

Mark

BIBLIOGRAPHY

Dobrosyzycki, Lucjan, *The Chronicle of the Lodz Ghetto 1941-1944*, (Yale University Press, 1984), 550 pp. Incredible anonymous entries documenting the daily ordeal suffered by the nearly 300,000 residents of the second largest ghetto in Poland, under the leadership of its controversial leader, Chaim Rumkowski. You feel the noose tightening.

Adelson, Alan, Lapides, Robert, *Lodz Ghetto: Inside a Community Under Siege*, (Viking Penguin, 1989) The sourcebook for the award-winning documentary film of the same title. An eye-opening view of the ghetto: "Listen and believe this. Even though it happened here. Even though it seems so old, so distant, and so strange." Jozef Zelkowicz

Grossman, Mendel, Smith, Frank Dabba, *My Secret Camera: Life in the Lodz Ghetto*, (Gulliver Books, 2000) A picture book with photographs taken by a concealed camera at the risk of his life.

Sierakowiak, Dawid, *The Diary of Dawid Sierakowiak*, Daily diary of a young man who died at age 19. The Anne Frank of Lodz.

Trunk, Isaiah, *Lodz Ghetto: A History*, translated by Robert Moses Shapiro (Published in Association with the United States Holocaust Memorial Museum, Indiana University Press, 2006) Most complete sourcebook for researching the Lodz ghetto.

ADDITIONAL RESOURCES

Photographs of the Lodz Ghetto by Mendel Grossman, David Ross, and other clandestine photographers helped provide background information for this book. Google "Lodz ghetto photographs." Many of these photographs were taken through holes in the photographers' coats, risking their lives.

United States Holocaust Museum: Visits to the museum helped provide the physical elements. I'm proud to be a supporter and invite you to join in their effort to combat hate and genocide for all people.

NEVER AGAIN TO ANYONE

More from NCG Key and Newhouse Creative Group

Visit NewhouseCreativeGroup.com for more from NCG Key and the rest of the Newhouse Creative Group family of authors.

About the Author

Born in Germany to Holocaust survivors, Mark loved teaching in Central Islip, Long Island, and was named Elementary/Secondary Teacher of the Year by the New York State Reading Association, among other honors. His mysteries for children, Welcome to Monstrovia; *The Case of the Disastrous Dragon*; and *The Case of the Crazy Chickenscratches* have won awards from Readers Favorite, The Benjamin Franklin Book Awards, The Florida Writers Association and others. *The Rockhound Science Mysteries* received Learning Magazines' Teachers' Choice Award. A former adjunct professor, Department of Education, SUNY, Old Westbury, he enjoys helping other writers and children, leading critique clubs and serving as the state Chairman of the Florida Writers Association Youth Program (FWAY). You may learn more about him and his books at www.newhousecreativegroup.com. He welcomes your comments, kind support, and reviews.

Made in the USA
Middletown, DE
24 November 2020